BEHIND ENEMY LINES
Evasion and Escape Aids of World War II

The catalog of the exhibition at The Frazier History Museum

Louisville, Kentucky
February – April, 2013

ELM GROVE PUBLISHING
San Antonio, Texas

Copyright © 2012 R.E. Baldwin. All rights reserved. No part of this work may be scanned, copied, uploaded or reproduced in any form or by any means, graphically, electronically or mechanically, without written permission from the copyright holder.

Images courtesy of the R.E. Baldwin Collection and the R.E. Baldwin – John A. Scott Map Collection except as noted.

ISBN: 978-1-943492-07-7

WWW.ELMGROVEPUBLISHING.COM

For Shirlaine

Acknowledgments

Thanks to Terrill Aitkin, Senior Curator of the National Museum of the United States Air Force, and to Ian Jenkins who retired after many years with the Australian War Memorial, for the years of friendship we have shared and for their unwavering support of this project.

Thanks to Madeleine Burnside, director of The Frazier History Museum, who saw promise in this exhibition and encouraged me to pursue it, to Kelly Williams, Curator of Collections, who led me through the process of turning an idea into reality, and to the tireless staff of the Frazier who took the unfamiliar material they received from me and in the space of less than a month turned it into something memorable.

Thanks to Mick Prodger for his friendship and generosity over many years, for sharing his expertise on all things aviation, and for his guidance and assistance in preparing this catalog for the museum.

Special thanks to my good friend John Stone of Louisville for being persistent in suggesting that I approach the Frazier about this exhibition, for his enthusiastic support of the project, and to him and his wife Kim for the Kentucky hospitality they have shown me on my yearly visits for more than two decades.

Eternal thanks to Shirlaine, my best friend and wife of more than 46-years, for all that is and ever has been good and true and beautiful in my life. She insisted, even through the difficult final days of her life, that I see the exhibition through to completion in spite of my sorrow.

R. E. Baldwin
February, 2013

Foreword to Second Edition

In 2012 I was invited by the Frazier History Museum in Louisville, Kentucky, to guest curate an exhibit of Second World War evasion and escape artifacts. The exhibit opened in February 2013 and enjoyed an extended run until April that same year, when it was disassembled and the items returned to private collections and storage.

The exhibit, which was entitled *Behind Enemy Lines*, showcased hundreds of items, most of which are seldom seen and had never previously been displayed together for public viewing.

Behind Enemy Lines was intended to be an introduction to the public of the work of the Evasion and Escape agencies of the Allies during World War II through the tangible remains of their effort. Artifacts were chosen to provide a representative cross-section of the evasion and escape aids produced by these agencies.

To accompany the exhibit, a full colour catalog featuring photographs and descriptions of all of the artifacts on display was produced. The catalog was intended solely as a photographic record of the exhibit, and is by no means a definitive work on the subject, but it has proven to be a popular reference source for collectors, historians and scholars, and so is now offered as a reprinted second edition which I hope readers will find both useful and informative.

R. E. Baldwin
September, 2015

Introduction

There are two distinct types of Evasion and Escape aids. The first are pre-capture aids, also called Evasion Aids. These were carried by service personnel in order to help them survive and avoid being captured by the enemy. The second are post-capture aids, also called Escape Aids. These were hidden to avoid detection by the enemy so that they could be used while under - and upon escape from - enemy control. They were hidden in parts of the uniform, and secreted in everyday objects carried by soldiers or sent into prison camps in specially marked parcels. Evasion Aids are far more plentiful than Escape Aids and make up the bulk of the exhibition.

I do not pretend to call myself an authority on all aspects of evasion and escape. My expertise is in language-related aids, with a good working knowledge of E&E maps, and I admit an affinity for the textiles. That said, I do have the research material and artifacts to assemble an exhibition such as this.

If I have done my job, you will acquire new respect for the remarkable E&E people who performed brilliantly in a field that was never envisioned before they set their hands to the work, inventing everything as the work progressed.

Except as noted, the images and artifacts depicted are from the R. E. Baldwin Collection. All maps are from the R. E. Baldwin - John A. Scott Map Collection, and represent but a fraction of the holdings

BEHIND ENEMY LINES
Evasion and Escape Aids of World War II

The dangers faced by soldiers trapped behind enemy lines has been recognized since the beginnings of warfare. Allied aircrew members, special operations personnel, and other soldiers at high risk of being caught behind enemy lines during World War II had a "secret weapon" unlike anything seen before. This weapon came in the form of the secret Evasion and Escape (E&E) organizations established first by the British government, and then by the United States. These organizations provided E&E training for Allied soldiers, organized safe escape routes in occupied countries, communicated with prisoners in enemy prisoner-of-war camps, and provided special E&E aids. It was an extraordinary operation, unique in military history, and inspired the Survival, Evasion, Rescue and Escape (SERE) operations conducted by today's military.

The Allied E&E effort during WWII was unparalleled in its scope. It came from a multitude of hastily created organizations staffed with extraordinary people who, with no prior experience, quickly learned, mastered, and perfected their craft. Their story, however, remains largely unknown and untold.

It is the purpose of this exhibit to bring this story to the public by introducing them to some of the artifacts that remain from that noble effort.

Winged Boot badge awarded to successful evaders and escapers.

George Washington's Passport

Long before the Second World War, in the earliest days of aviation, people recognized the hazards to strangers arriving suddenly and unannounced in a flying machine amongst people they do not know. When, in 1793, Jean-Pierre Blanchard, Europe's pre-eminent balloonist who spoke little to no English, lifted off from Philadelphia on the first piloted balloon flight in America accompanied by a small dog, he carried with him a "Passport" written by President George Washington to provide for his safety upon his landing. In his book about the flight, Blanchard writes that when he landed in New Jersey he was impressed by the respect that the citizens had for President Washington when a farmer read the passport to the crowd who had gathered. This was the first known use of a language aid designed specifically for use by an aviator.

French Balloonist Jean-Pierre Blanchard, who made the first piloted flight in America in 1793.
Public Domain image from the National Archives

Title page from Blanchard's book, showing his balloon
from "The First Air Voyage in America"

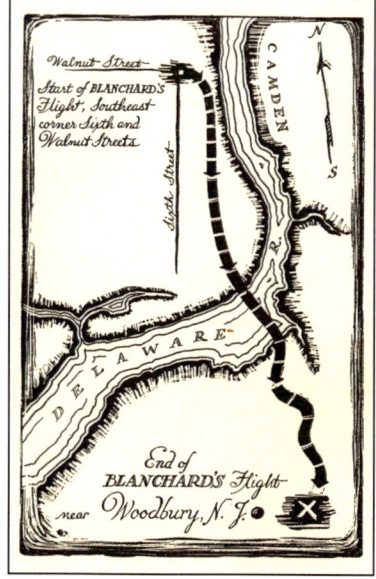

The route of Blanchard's balloon voyage
from "The First Air Voyage in America"

> * **GEORGE WASHINGTON**, *President of the United States of America,*
>
> TO ALL TO WHOM THESE PRESENTS SHALL COME.
>
> THE bearer hereof, Mr. Blanchard a citizen of France, proposing to ascend in a balloon from the city of Philadelphia, at 10 o'clock, A. M. this day, to pass in such direction and to descend in such place as circumstances may render most convenient—THESE are therefore to recommend to all citizens of the United States, and others, that in his passage, descent, return or journeying elsewhere, they oppose no hindrance or molestation to the said Mr. Blanchard; And, that on the contrary, they receive and aid him with that humanity and good will, which may render honor to their country, and justice to an individual so distinguished by his efforts to establish and advance an art, in order to make it useful to mankind in general.
>
> Given under my hand and seal at the city of Philadelphia, this ninth day of January, one thousand seven hundred and ninety three, and of the independence of America the seventeenth.
>
> (Seal.)
>
> Signed GEORGE WASHINGTON.

The text of the Passport given to Blanchard by President Washington
from "The First Air Voyage in America"

Images from "The First Air Voyage in America" by Jean Pierre Blanchard
are provided compliments of Applewood Books, Carlisle, MA: www.awb.com

FAI Certificates

The Fédération Aéronatuique Internationale (FAI) was founded in Paris in October 1905. In November the Aero Club of America, the FAI's representative in the U.S., was founded in New York. The FAI set standards for pilots and issued certificates to pilots who met these standards beginning in 1909. Recognizing that aviation events were often international, the FAI included requests for assistance in six European languages on the last two pages of its certificates. Countries that were not FAI members sometimes adopted the format of the FAI certificate for their own pilot certificates, including the requests for assistance in various languages. Two examples of these certificates are shown here.

This FAI Certificate was issued to Lt. W. A. Gates of Louisville, Kentucky, by the Aero Club of America in 1918. The request for assistance in six European languages is on the last two pages. Lt. Gates survived the war and returned to Louisville.

Though badly damaged, this certificate is significant because it shows that the importance of aviators being to communicate in other languages was recognized in Asia well before World War Two. This Siamese Army Certificate of Aviator was issued to Corporal Hang Jum-sum-ran in 1929. Though not an FAI certificate, it is clearly a similar form, including the request for assistance in six languages on the last two pages.

The 1914-1918 War

World War One was characterized by a lack of official interest in Evasion and Escape. In many cases, Allied pilots were forbidden to carry identification, so even the simple request for assistance printed at the back of their FAI Certificates would have been unavailable.

Late in the war, British flyers who managed to evade or escape from German hands were used to deliver lectures to airmen, but aviators were basically left to fend for themselves. In his book *Legion of the Lafayette* (Doubleday, 1962), Arch Whitehouse described how he and other airmen prepared for the possibility of capture by putting small items like a compass in the hollowed-out heel of a boot, concealng small hacksaw blades in the seams of their jackets, and hiding other items such as knife blades and pieces of mirror for signaling in their gear.

Some airmen carried small silk flags for patriotic purposes, but they would also have been useful when approaching Allied lines or French civilians.

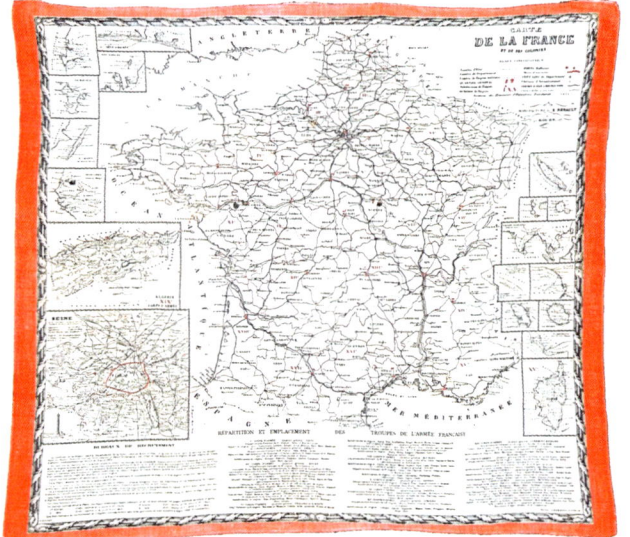

Small-scale maps like this one of France could be hidden in a pilot's clothing, but would have been of limited use due to the lack of detail.

A Corporal Bousquet wore this cloth map of France as a scarf. Similar maps could have proved useful to evading pilots.

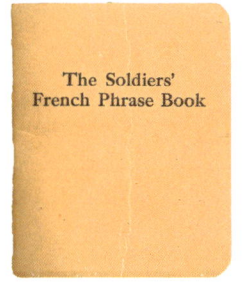
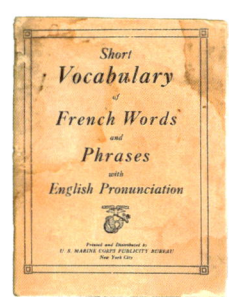
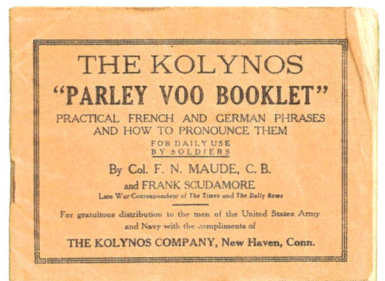

Many phrase books were printed by patriotic companies and organizations and given to soldiers going overseas. Any of these could easily have been carried in an aircraft.

Policing an Empire

The British used aircraft to police their far-flung Empire because aircraft offered a more effective and economical means of controlling populations than sending foot soldiers. In India, the British faced tribes that were accustomed to taking enemy prisoners for ransom. What was originally called a Ransom Note was devised to convince tribesmen that airmen were valuable in order to spare them from torture. Because torture could involve the removal of the "family jewels," aircrews referred to Ransom Notes as Goolie Chits, goolie being the Hindustani word for ball, and chit being an IOU. These were the first language aids developed by the military of any nation specifically for use by airmen.

The first recorded use of Goolie Chits was by 31 Squadron, in early 1917 in the Northwest Frontier Province of India, and it was not long until their use spread to other parts of the Empire. The Goolie Chit became the Blood Chit, blood signifying life, because goolie was not a word that could be used in polite company, or, it seems, in official correspondence.

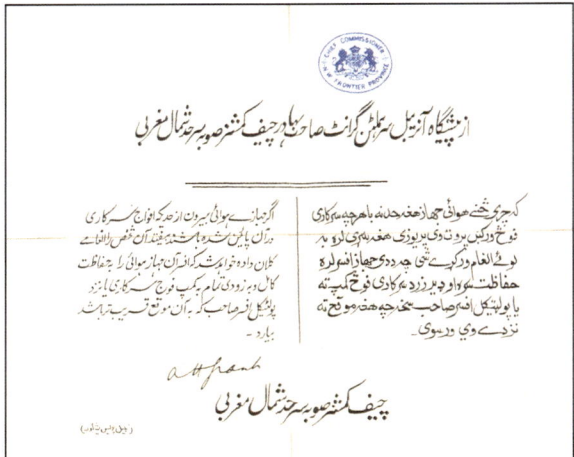

Facsimile of what is thought to be one of the earliest Goolie Chits. Written in Farsi on the left side and Pashto on the right, it was known to have been issued in quantity by 1919.

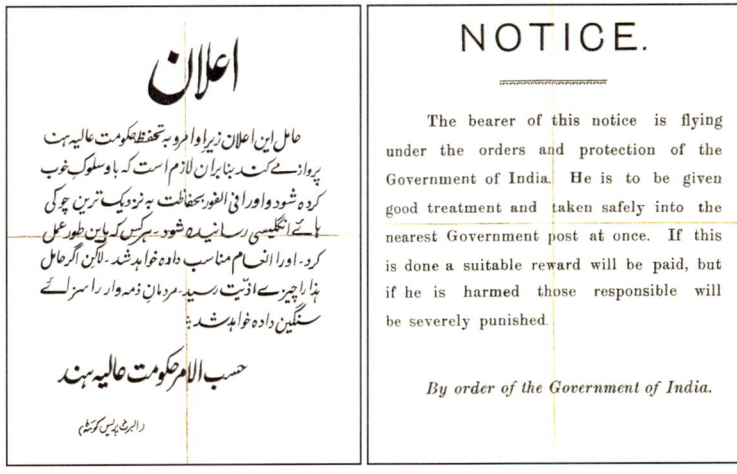

This facsimile of an early two-sided Goolie Chit is written in Farsi and English.

Two original Goolie Chits from Mesopotamia (Iraq), circa 1919. These were issued to Capt. S. L. Pettis, RAF, in the smaller envelope, and carried by him in his aircraft in the larger envelope marked "Arabic Protection Letter." Capt. Pettis was captured and lost an eye.

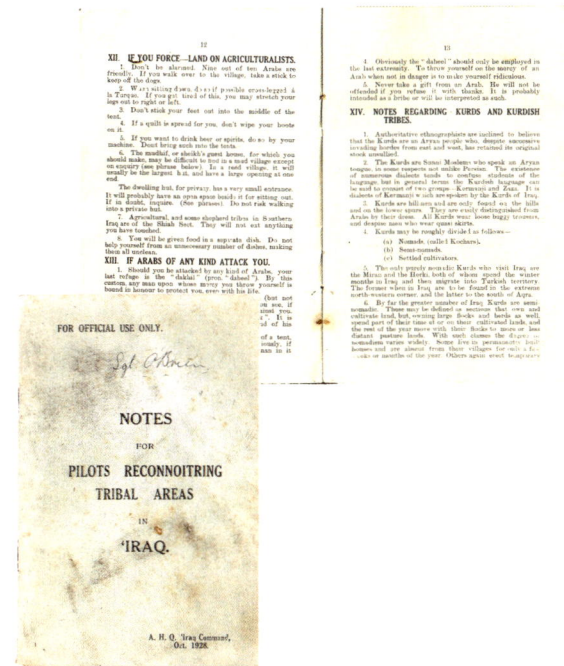

In addition to Goolie Chits, booklets like this one issued to a Sgt. O'Brien were provided to aircrews. It contains cultural information and instructions on what to do if forced down among the various peoples of Iraq.

Chinese-Americans in China

Some Chinese-American pilots, who in the 1920s and 1930s were denied a career in aviation in the United States because of their ethnicity, instead found one in China. When Japan invaded Manchuria, many made the transition to military aviation in the Chinese and Cantonese Air Forces, while others ferried war material with civilian companies. Other pilots went to China in 1937 and 1938 after Japan invaded the rest of China. Although some spoke only English, no language aids were provided to them. This would change with the arrival of more American and European pilots in 1938.

Perhaps the best-known Chinese-American volunteers are the group from Portland, Oregon, who had joined the Chinese Air Force by 1935.

Despite flying obsolete aircraft, many of them biplanes, Chinese-Americans in the Chinese Air Force became the first American "aces" in what would become the Second World War, before other Americans flew with the Royal Air Force "Eagle Squadrons."

The Fourteenth Squadron

In October 1937 a squadron of foreign volunteers was formed by a decision of Madame Chiang Kai-shek, under the guidance of Col. Claire Lee Chennault. The unit, the 14th Volunteer Bombardment Squadron of the Chinese Air Force, had 11 American, European and Australian pilots plus 16 Chinese air gunners. Because the foreigners could not speak Chinese, a cloth patch called a Hu Chao, or Rescue Patch, was provided to them for use in the event that they were forced down.

This Rescue Patch, like those issued to the 14th Squadron, pre-dates the First American Volunteer Group (A.V.G.). Its form and function are the prototype for the Rescue Patches and Blood Chits that would follow.

American pilots George Weigle and Elwyn H. Gibbon of the 14th Squadron pose for a photo in the winter of 1937-38. Weigle is wearing his Rescue Patch on the front of his flight suit.
Image courtesy of the San Diego Air & Space Museum
http://www.sandiegoairandspace.org/

The American Volunteer Group

Although the 14th Squadron lasted only a few months, their successors in 1941, the American Volunteer Group (A.V.G.) of the Chinese Air Force became immortalized in the collective mind of America as the Flying Tigers. They symbolize the American character, a blend of compassion, self-sacrifice, and a willingness to help defend others from aggression and tyranny.

The first A.V.G. Rescue Patches were issued to pilots of the 1st and 2nd Squadrons Kunming, China, on Christmas Day 1941. Members of the 3rd Squadron, who had stayed behind in Burma, received their Rescue patches when they arrived in Kunming in January 1942.

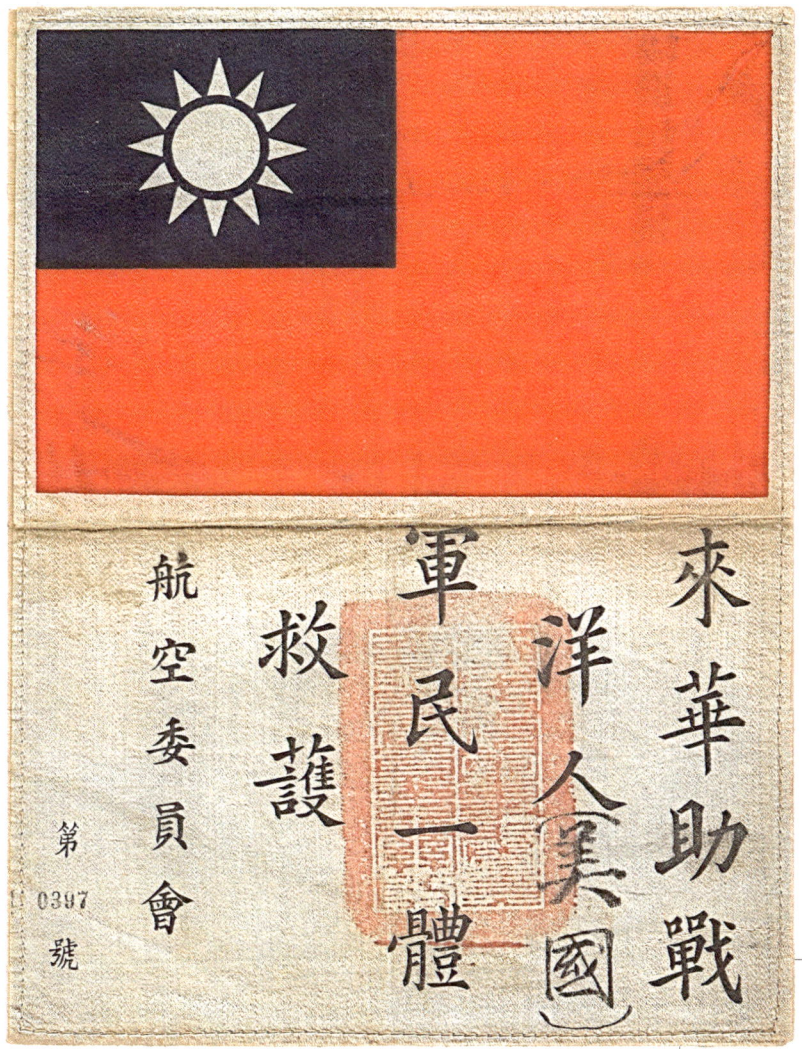

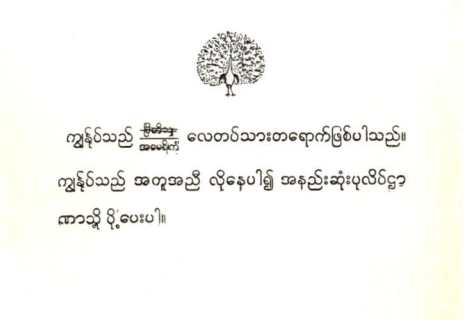

Facsimile of the first goolie chit issued to members of the A.V.G. These were given to them upon their arrival in Burma by the British.

Above: One of two general types of Rescue Patches issued to the A.V.G., this example is distinguished by having two characters next to the serial number. A characteristic of all A.V.G. Rescue Patches is that the chop (red stamp) of China's Aeronautical Commission, headed by Madame Chiang-kai Shek, is more or less centered in the text.

Right: Members of the A.V.G at a pre-flight meeting. Pilots are wearing their Rescue Patches on the back of their flight suits.
Image courtesy of Ron Burkey, Flying Tiger Antiques
www. http://flyingtigerantiques.com/

A second version type of A.V.G. Rescue Patch was acquired by Henry Johnson when he arrived in Kunming. It has three characters next to the serial number, and lacks the characters in parentheses denoting "America." Its serial number 0548 is at the upper limit of the numbers issued to A.V.G. members.

These photos and an A.V.G. banner were acquired from Henry Johnson along with his Rescue Patch. Johnson, a technical representative for an American aircraft company, arrived in Kunming around the time the A.V.G. was being disbanded. The photos show him with a P-40B of the A.V.G., and a newer model P-40 awaiting use by the newly formed China Air Task Force in the background

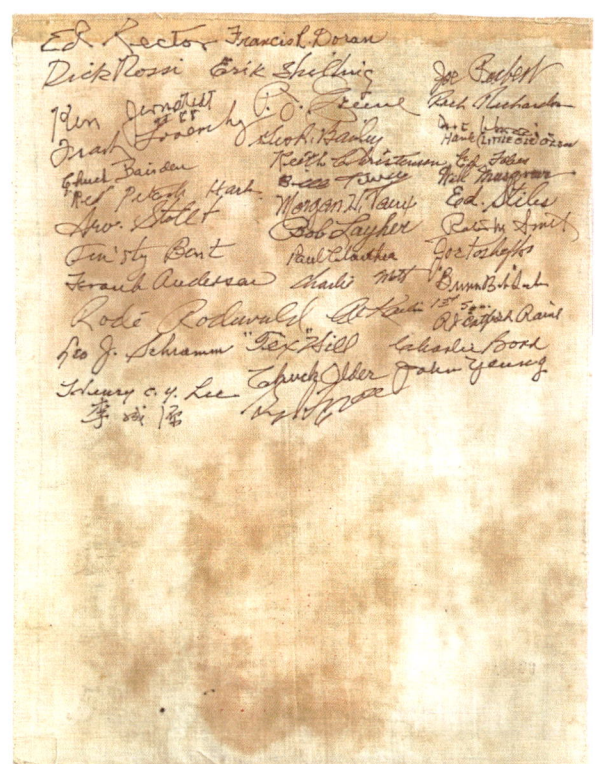

Chinese Rescue Patches are typically printed on silk and sewn to cotton backing, as shown here. The back of this un-issued A.V.G. Rescue Patch has been signed by 38 members of the group, plus C. Y. "Henry" Lee, Chennault's Chinese Air Force interpreter.

On 4 July 1942 the A.V.G. was disbanded. Its members were given discharge certificates like the one above that was issued to Crew Chief Robert A. Smith.

World War Two

The war that began when Japan invaded China in 1931 grew into a world conflict on 1 September 1939 when Germany invaded Poland. Britain's Agreement of Mutual Assistance with Poland brought the country into the war.

The U.S. remained neutral as Germany invaded European countries and the Soviet Union. On 7 December 1942 the Empire of Japan attacked the Pacific Fleet at Pearl Harbor, bringing the US into the war.

World War II eventually affected 104 countries and every continent except Antarctica.

Because much of WWII was fought in the air, the fate of air crews forced down in enemy-held territory became of great concern. In December 1939, Britain created the Directorate of Military Intelligence Section 9 (MI9) to oversee Evasion and Escape (E&E) efforts to assist and recover air crews and others in particular danger of being captured behind enemy lines, and to aid those who had been captured. MI9 was headquartered in Room 424 at the Metropole on Northumberland Avenue. P-Branch gave training to air crews and others such as SOEoperatives, while E-Branch operated patrols behind enemy lines and established escape routes.

The United States had no E&E agency when it entered the war, but in February 1942 the Americans were introduced to MI9's well-functioning program and anAmerican staff branch, P/W&X, began working with MI9. In October 1942 the US formed the CPM branch of G2, which established the Military Intelligence Service E&E Section, MIS-X, which was headquartered at Fort Hunt, Virginia. MIS-X often went by the even more cryptic name "PO Box 1142," its mailing address. Its first commander, Col. Robley Winfrey, received five months of training at MI9 prior to taking the command of the unit.

In May 1943, MI9 and MIS-X came to an agreement to share resources and divide responsibilities. Europe, India, and South East Asia became the responsibility of Britain. The US became resposible for China, Indochina, the South West Pacific Area, Japan, and Eastern Siberia. In North Africa responsibilities were shared. This explains why American personnel in Europe were issued British E&E aids, and why Commonwealth personnel in the Pacific received American E&E aids.

These E&E agencies and their sub-sections fanned out across the globe. In October 1941, GS I(e) was established in New Delhi, India. Later, in the autumn of 1943, GS I(e) and MIS-X Technical Section India formed the a joint agency, E-Group, which operated out of Assam, India, and Ceylon. In Hong Kong the British Army Aid Group (BAAG) was organized. In North Africa, N-Section of A-Force, which originally handled E&E activities in Africa and the Mediterranean, split into IS9 (CMF) to coordinate E&E in Albania, Yugoslavia, and the central Mediterranean and IS9 (ME) operating in the Middle East. In China, MIS-X established the Air Ground Aid Section (AGAS), and the MIS-X South West Pacific Area Section in Brisbane covered Australia, New Zealand, the Philippine Islands, Netherlands East Indies, and many smaller islands. In November 1944, MIS-X established its Pacific Ocean Area (POA) section on Guam.

That these agencies operated in so many different areas, all of them procuring at least some of their materials locally, explains in part the enormous variety in the E&E aids in this exhibition.

Per Ardua Libertas

Christopher Clayton Hutton, the genius behind many of MI9's "gadget" E&E aids, produced a few copies of a book that he titled *Per Ardua Libertas*, Latin for "Through Adversity to Freedom," as a record of MI9's work on escape aids over the course of its first two years. Copies of this book were said to have been placed on a large mahogany table in a secure room for review for the American mission visiting England under the command of Maj. Gen. Carl Spattz in February 1942, where they provided Americans with a first glimpse of Britain's comprehensive E&E program.

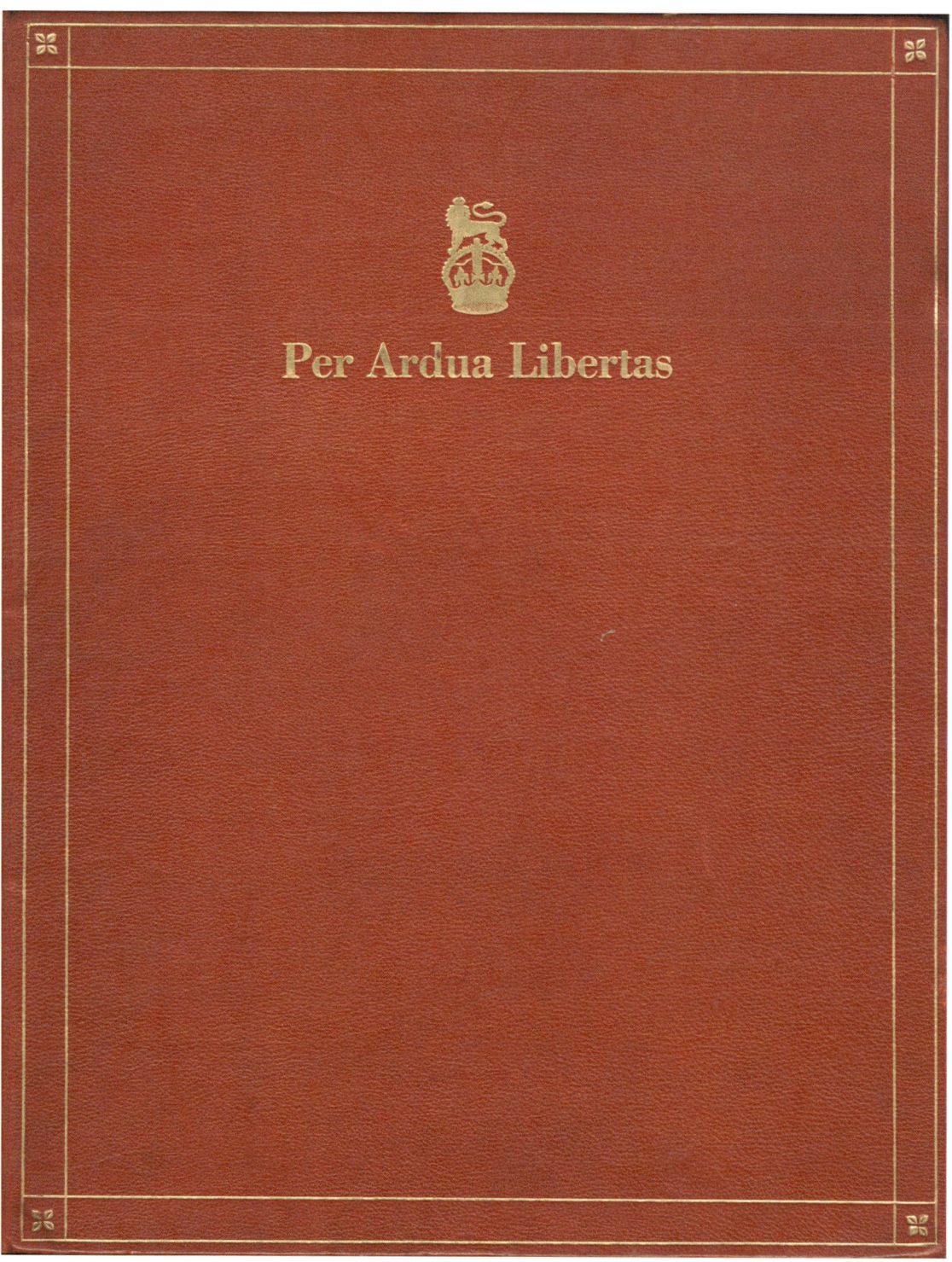

The cover of this handmade book is made of Moroccan leather. It introduced the American military to Evasion and Escape by revealing the workings of MI9, Britain's E&E agency.

```
                                    War Office,
                                    London, S.W.1.
                                    14.2.1942.

              NOTE.

       The following pages give a photographic
  review of the range of work I was privileged
  to be entrusted with on behalf of Section
  M.I.9, for two years between February 14th, 1940,
  and February 14th, 1942.

       They show "Aids to Escape" - Pre-Capture and
  Post-Capture - and in addition show various other
  articles called for by various Sections of the
  three Services which, through the channels laid on,
  M.I.9, were enabled to produce or deliver quickly.

       No details are given in this review of the
  difficulties experienced in obtaining manufacture
  of the various Aids.  These are dealt with in
  separate notes—as are the names of the manufacturers.

       Two points, perhaps, should be put on
  record.  During the period covered, no finished
  working suggestion was ever submitted to me by
  any other Service Department and no Service Factory
  or Organisation was used in the manufacture of
  any article.

       I should like to record my sincere thanks to
  Colonel N. R. Crockatt, D.S.O., M.C., for his kindly
  understanding of the very difficult problems with
  which I was faced and for the considerable latitude
  he has always granted me in letting me work in my
  own irregular way; without such help the results
  shown in this book could never have been so
  effectively achieved.

       With but few exceptions, all articles were
  devised and production obtained by me.

                                C. Clayton Hutton
                                      Major.
```

Christopher Clayton Hutton, the genius behind many of Britain's E&E aids, explains the purpose of his book *Per Ardua Libertas* on a sheet of War Office stationery that is affixed to a page in the book.

The Charter.

CONDUCT OF WORK No. 48.
M.I.9.

1. A new section of the Intelligence Directorate at the War Office has been formed. It will be called M.I.9. It will work in close connection with and act as agent for the Admiralty and Air Ministry.

2. The Section is responsible for:—

   (a) The preparation and *execution* of plans for facilitating the escape of British Prisoners of War of all three Services in Germany or elsewhere.

   (b) Arranging instruction in connection with above.

   (c) Making other advance provision, as considered necessary.

   (d) Collection and dissemination of information obtained from British Prisoners of War.

   (e) Advising on counter-escape measures for German Prisoners of War in Great Britain, if requested to do so.

3. M.I.9. will be accommodated in Room 424, Metropole Hotel.

(Sgd.) J. SPENCER.
Col. G.S.
for D.M.I.

23.12.39.

The official mission of MI9 is explained.

ARTIFICIAL SILK MAPS

(Waterproofed 'Tenasco')

●

Double-sided

●

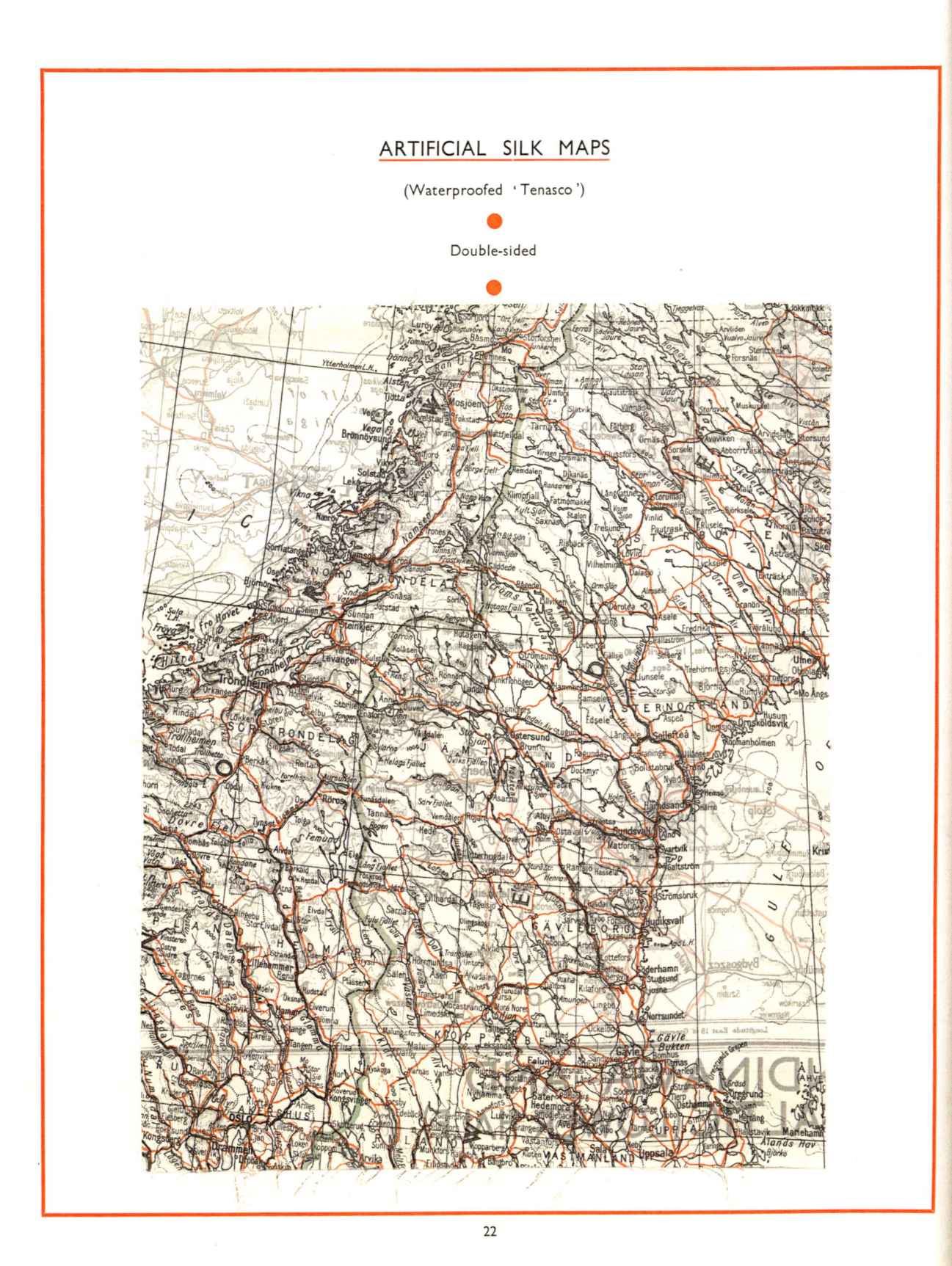

Pieces of actual cloth and tissue paper maps made of various materials are attached to some of the pages.

Left: Escape compasses.

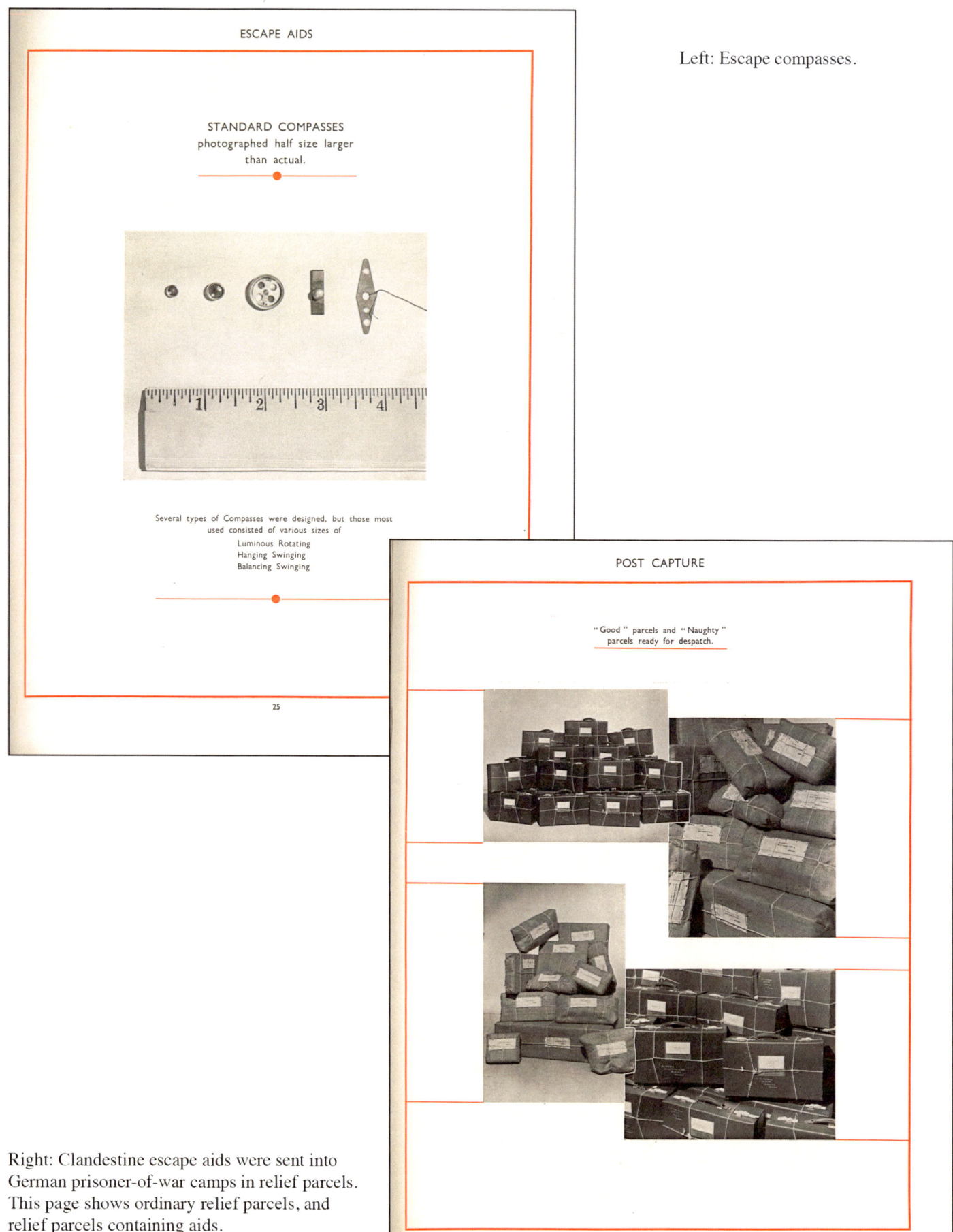

Right: Clandestine escape aids were sent into German prisoner-of-war camps in relief parcels. This page shows ordinary relief parcels, and relief parcels containing aids.

ANOTHER NAME FOR M.I.9

●

PRISONERS' LEISURE HOURS FUND

*"The treasures to be found in idle hours—
only those who seek may find."*
Runyan.

President:
B. ATTENBOROUGH, Esq.

Vice-Presidents:
Sir THOMAS BERNEY, Bart.
L. C. UNDERHILL, Esq.

Committee:
Lady D. BROWNE.
The Hon. Mrs. E. FREEMAN.
P. O. NORTON, Esq.
J. B. WORLES, Esq.

66 BOLT COURT,
FLEET STREET,
LONDON, E.C.4.

Hon. Treasurer:
E. TOWNSEND, Esq., C.A.

Hon. Secretary:
Miss FREDA MAPPIN.

Telephone:
CENTRAL 3951

12th MAY, 1941

Dear Sir,

    Through the kindness of one of our contributors, we are enabled to send to you a selection of Musical Instruments - and Gramophone Records, and we are having despatched direct from the manufacturers in the course of a few days some records.

    We intend despatching different selections for each prisoner of war - to whom we send these, and it is hoped in order that all may enjoy the variety, you will offer to interchange with each other.

    Further supplies will be sent you at regular intervals, and if there is any particular record you desire sent, perhaps you will look through the Catalogues we are sending letting us know the make and number, and we will do our best to despatch to you in due course.

    Trusting you are enjoying good health, and looking on the bright side of things.

    Yours faithfully,

    Secretary.

A Voluntary Fund formed for the purpose of sending Comforts, Games, Books, etc. to British Prisoners of War.

50

Red cross parcels were not used to send clandestine aids into POW camps because it would compromise the work of the Red Cross. Instead, dummy aid organizations were established to send aid parcels. A sample letter on the stationery of one of these dummy organizations is glued to a page of *Per Ardua Libertas*.

Official Blood Chits

The blood chits in this display were issued by the Allies to their servicemen. Some owe their lineage to the earlier Ransom Notes issued in India and Rescue Patches issued in China, while some depart from those themes. Some offer a reward for the safe return of the bearer, and some do not. They are purposely arranged in a random, non-chronological order to encourage readers to compare them and discover both similarities and differences. Blood Chits are Evasion (pre-capture) Aids. Items noted * were removed from the exhibition due to space limitations and are shown here courtest of the Virtual Frazier feature.

"He continued up the stream-bed for what he estimates as two miles. Then, as he was resting, he observed a Chinese walking along near by and hailed him. The Chinese was startled and frightened at first but he understood the situation immediately when he was shown the Chinese Back Flag [Blood Chit]."
- Walkout Report of Capt. Kenneth E. George, 76th Fighter Squadron, 23rd Fighter Group, 25 February 1944

Left: This Blood chit belonged to John L. Cella, Escape and Evasion Officer and Search and Rescue of the 20th Bomber Command. The third character in the right hand column of text has been changed from earlier blood chits. Silk with cotton backing.
Right: Blood chit in 16 Asian languages. There are several styles of this type, known as DEB-11 in Asia. Rayon-acetate.

Left: The camels on this Burmese blood chit represent flights over the "Hump," that is across the Himalaya mountains from India to China. There are more camels stamped on the back. Silk with cotton backing.
Right: US-made blood chit patterned after an earlier one printed in India, written in Chinese plus four languages found in Burma. Rayon-acetate.

Left: MIS-X "Type 1" blood chit* in Chinese, so-named because of the number 1 in the lower right corner. It is patterned after an earlier blood chit issued by China. The "W" denotes that it is issued in Washington, D.C. Rayon-acetate (cupramonium).

Center: MIS-X "Type 2" blood chit in Chinese signed by Carl N. Peterson and Lloyd R. Shoemaker, the two MIS-X personnel assigned to stamp the "chop" (red stamp) on the blood chits in the Chinese Embassy in Washington, D.C. Rayon acetate.

Right: MIS-X "Type 3" blood chit* written in Chinese plus four languages found in Burma, patterned after earlier blood chits printed in both the US and India. Rayon-acetate.

Above: MIS-X "Type 4" blood chit in 7 languages used in Asia. The Japanese language was intended for use in Korea rather than in Japan where a blood chit would have been useless. Rayon-acetate,

Right: Blood chit issued to Boatswain's Mate Bruce Peterson of SACO. Though it appears to be a souvenir-type blood chit, it was officially issued to Peterson and bears the chop giving it the required authority. SACO was the U.S. Navy presence in China, a joint Chinese and American group sometimes called the "Rice Paddy Navy." Pieced silk with cotton backing.

  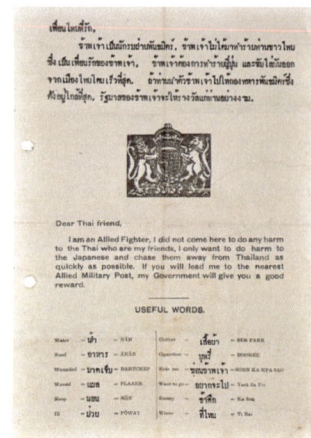

Left: One of the most complete blood chits issued in North Africa. This British example not only has a message in Arabic, but also points on conduct, useful words and phrases, and hints on desert travel. Paper with linen backing.

Center: The only known type of blood chit issued by the Soviet Union, this one was brought back by a member of the US Military Mission in Moscow. The message is indeed that of a blood chit and the names J. (Josef) Stalin and A. (Gen. Alekseia) Antonov in the lower right corner give it authority. There is no evidence that this type of blood chit was issued to air crews. Cotton.

Right: Blood chit in Thai, including useful words at the bottom. Paper with linen backing.

Left: Two-sided blood chit issued to participants of Operation Frantic, where the Allies bombed Germany, refueled and re-armed in the Soviet Union, and bombed Germany again on their return to home bases. This side was to be held with both hands over one's head when approaching Soviet troops. Artificial silk (Tenasco).

Center: An early blood chit in Arabic issued to a Sergeant Smith. Paper with linen backing.

Right: Blood chit known as DEB-10, printed in India. Chinese and four languages found in Burma. Silk with cotton backing.

  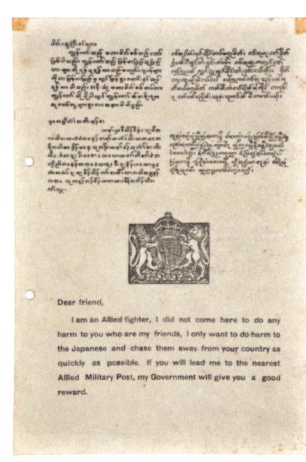

Left: Blood chit in 17 languages for use in Asia. Artificial silk.

Center: An example of the very first MIS-X blood chit, in six languages for us in Asia. Serial numbers began at 20,000. Cotton.

Right: Blood chit for use in Burma. Paper with linen backing.

  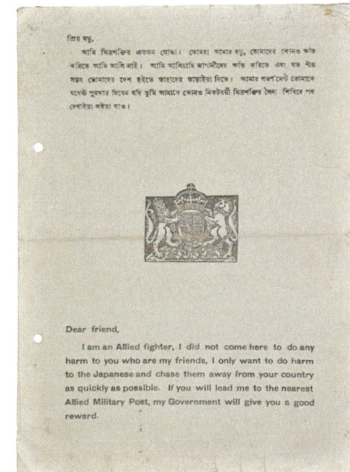

Left: An un-issued A.V.G. Rescue Patch* that was issued to air crews arriving in China following the disbandment of the A.V.G., as shown in the photo* next to it. Silk with cotton backing.

Right: Blood chit in Bengali for use in India. Paper with linen backing.

Above: Early 17-language blood chit for Asia printed in India. It has been serial numbered by hand. Silk.

Left: Like the SACO blood chit elsewhere in this exhibit, this CNAC blood chit may appear to be a souvenir type blood chit because it was locally produced in China, but it was indeed officially issued. It was numbered by the Chinese National Aviation Corporation, and bears a chop to give it the required authority. This blood chit belonged to Captain Kirkpatrick, whose nicname was "Captain Kirk." Pieced cotton.

Left: Blood chit printed by the US Government Printing Office specifically for crews of the Air Transport Command ferrying aircraft from the US to the European theater and North Africa. Paper.

Center: This blood chit in Pidgin English was issued to Lt. Col N. W. Pratt of Marine Air Group 25, stationed on Vella Lavella Island in the Solomons. The top message was used by persons who can read, and the bottom message was to be read by the airman to persons who could not read. Paper.

Right: Two-sided blood chit for use when approaching Soviet troops. This side gives instructions on how it is to be used. Not all blood chits offered a reward for the return of a downed airman, but all served essentially the same purpose of saving the airman's life. Artificial silk.

Left: Folded blood chit for use in North Africa in the form of a Passport with a message from President Roosevelt. The outside of the card is at the top, the inside at the bottom. Cardstock.

Right: Blood chit in the Amharic language for use by RAF crews flying against Italian targets in Ethiopia, with the stamp of Emperor Haile Selasse, whose photo is with the blood chit. Linen.

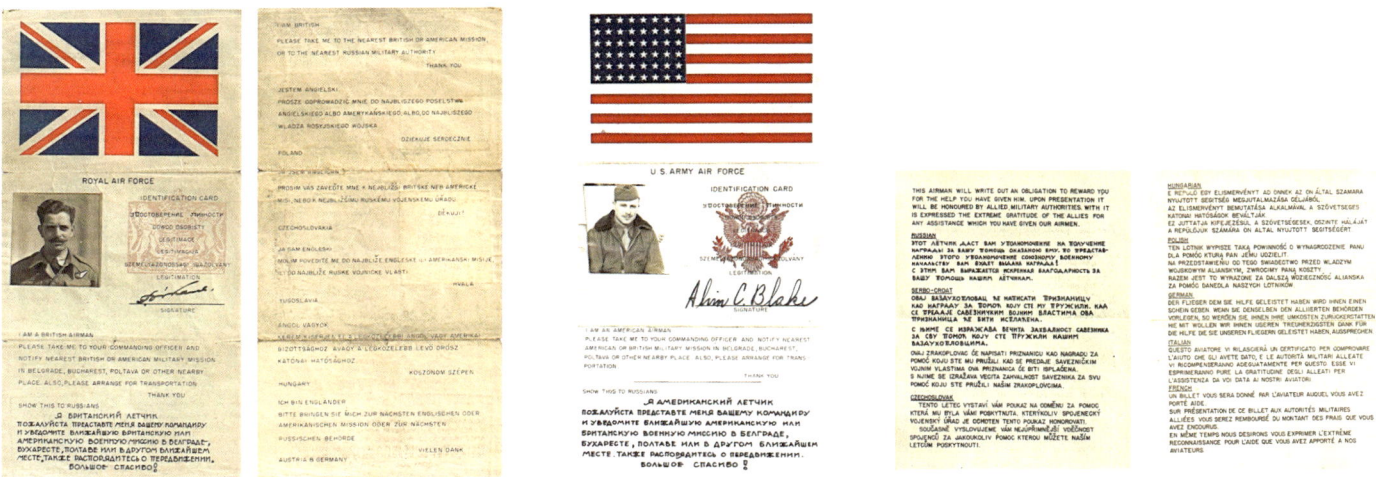

Left: This 2-sided combination identification card and blood chit in 6-languages was issued to Patrick O'Kane of 104 Squadron.
Center: This American version of the 2-sided 6-language blood chit was issued to Alvin C. Blake of the 15th A.F.
Right: This type of 2-sided blood chit in 9-languages was often issued with the 6-language blood chits to its left.

Left: Blood Chits for Operation Frantic were often worn around the neck in acetate sleeves like this.

Right: This paper version of the Operation Frantic blood chit was issued with a phrase card in a cellophane envelope.

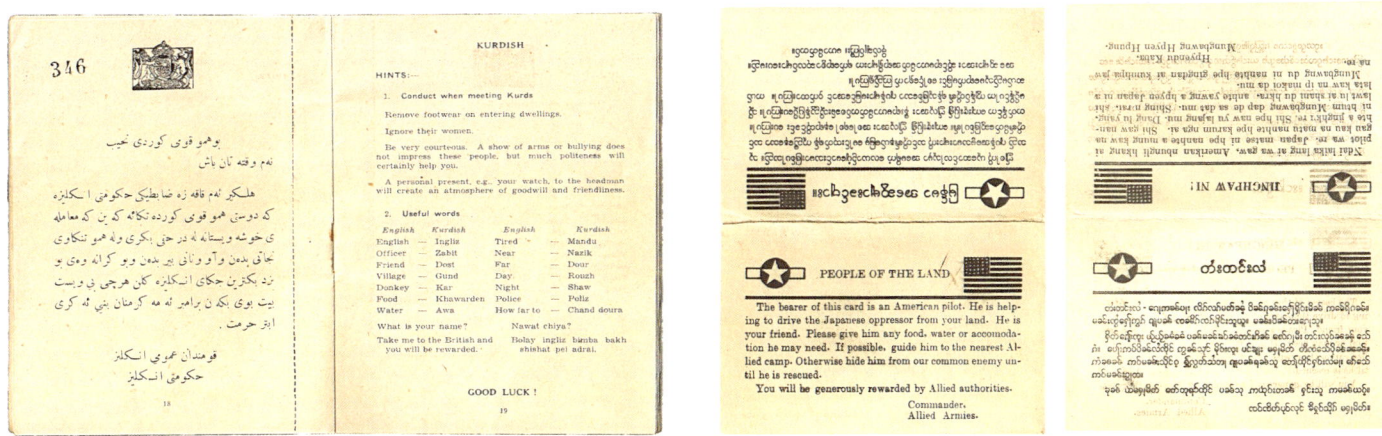

Left: This booklet of tear-out-blood chits in 6-languages for North Africa was printed by Middle East Forces (M.E.F.)
Right: 2-sided card blood chit for use in the Shan States, Burma.

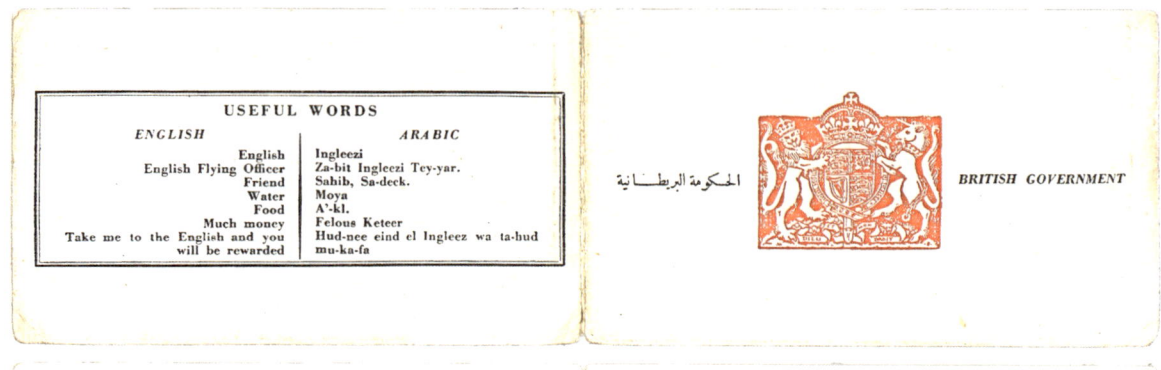

Above: Folded card blood chit for use by British troops in North Africa. A propaganda forgery of this card with the same English message but an insulting arabic message was made by the Germans.

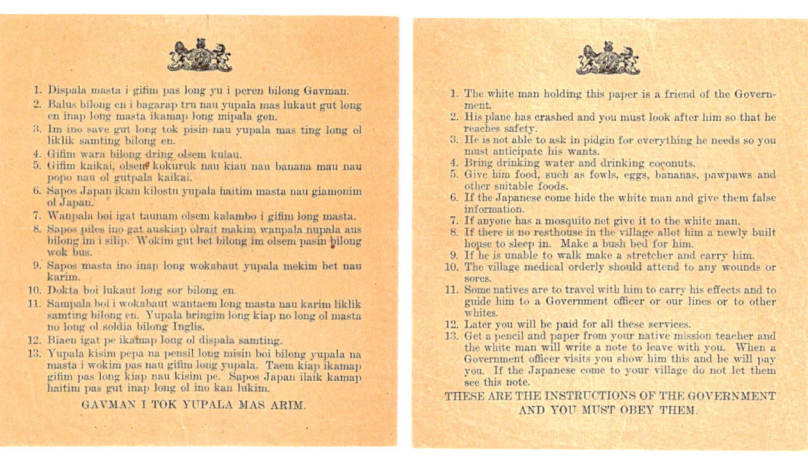

Two-sided newsprint blood chit in Pidgin English and English for use in the South West Pacific.

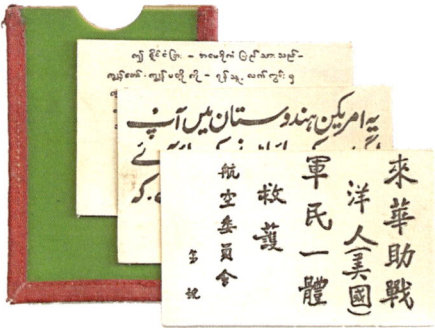
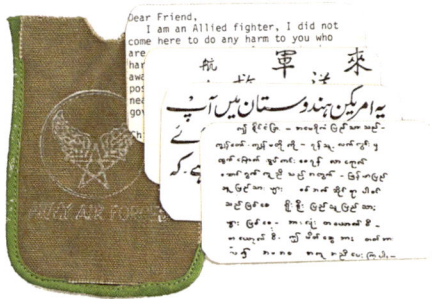
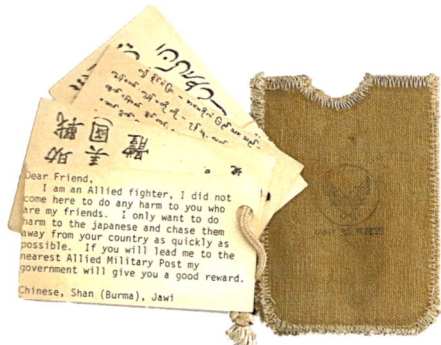

Above: Four sets of blood chits on cards for use in India, China, and Burma illustrate the variety that a single, simple idea like this could spawn. These cards were known in Asia as DEB-1.

"Climbing a steep hill, the flyers came upon several Chinese boys, several of whom apparently understood enough of the writing on the Chinese blood chit the flyers were wearing to point out a direction."
- *Bulletin on Escape and Evasion No. 10, 20th Bomber Command, 8 September 1944*

Unofficial Blood Chits

Entrepreneurs in Asia were quick to recognize the monetary potential in modifying existing cloth items into blood chits, and even more the potential for locally made blood chits. In addition, airmen felt free to personalize them, something they were less likely to do with government issued blood chits. Leather versions were particularly durable and highly desirable for sewing onto the backs of flight jackets until the practice was forbidden. Most were copies of official blood chits, but some original designs also appeared. As souvenirs and patches they did not carry government approval, but the quality of craftsmanship of some made them highly desirable and some people did carry them on missions, so in an odd way they may qualify as Evasion (pre-capture) Aids.

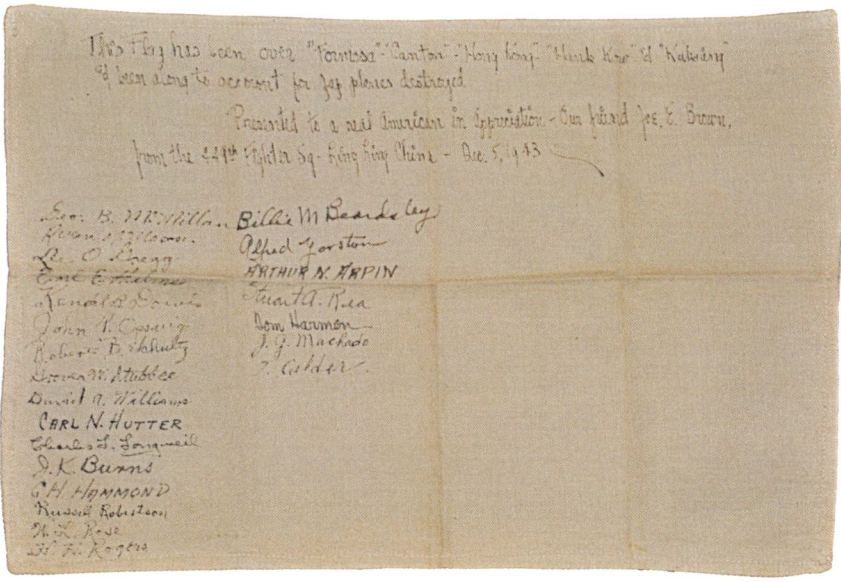

Above: The flag was printed on silk and sewn to cotton backing in India and officially issued to flyers. Some, like this one, were converted into blood chits by hiring someone to write the text on them.

Right: The front of this blood chit is similar but not identical to the one shown to its left. It was given to Joe E. Brown by the 449th Fighter Squadron when he was entertaining the troops in China, and is signed by 23 of its members. The squadron flew P-38 aircraft and its members included a number of notable pilots. Among the signatures are those of former Vice-Squadron Leader of the A.V.G.'s 3rd Squadron, George B. McMillen, Billie M. Beardsley, who is credited with shooting down one of the top Japanese generals, and by football great Tom Harmon.

Left: Silk appliqué with printed sun symbol and handwritten text.
Center: Leather appliqué version of an official issue blood chit for Burma, with handwritten text.
Right: Silk appliqué and embroidered piece done by someone not familiar with writing Chinese. Thought to have been made in the Philippine Islands.

Left: This leather appliqué chit belonged to Wm. Conelley, whose name appears on the flag. He drew stylized mountains on it to record his Hump missions, and made notations on the missions with various symbols whose meaning are no longer known.

Right: Leather appliqué chit with and embroidery and handwritten text for naval personnel.

Left: Beautiful silk appliqué and embroidery with handwritten text.
Center: Silk appliqué with embroidered sun and fully embroidered text.
Right: Silk appliqué with hand written text including owners name and a reasonable translation of the Chinese.

Left: Leather appliqué with handwritten text. The stylized American flag covers the entire left of the chit.
Right: Leather appliqué with handwritten text. The chit is long enough that the flags assume rather normal proportions.

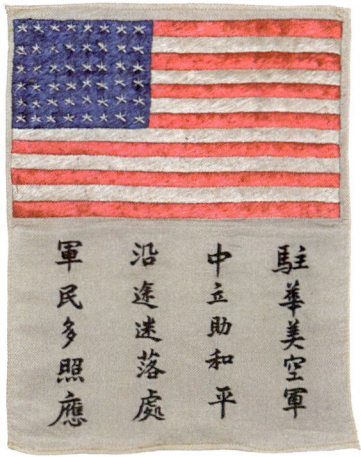 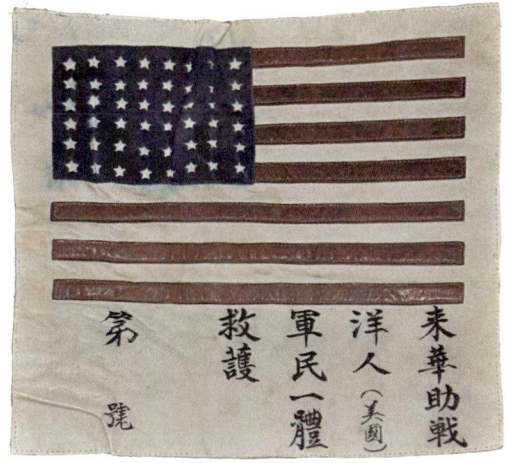 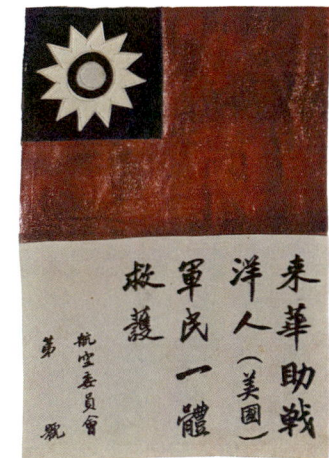

Left: Fully embroidered silk American flag and Chinese text.
Center: Leather appliqué American flag with handwritten text.
Right: A leather appliqué copy of the standard-issue A.V.G Rescue Patch with handwritten text.

Left: Beautifully designed Burmese blood chit printed on silk.
Right: Nationalist Chinese flag with blood chit text printed on cotton. The owner's name, Col. Gerry Mason, has been added. The additional text written on the back shows through to the front.

Left: Fully embroidered silk flag and text.
Center: Large appliqué leather flag.
Right: Extremely small appliqué leather shoulder patch, illustrating the souvenir nature of these articles.

One-of-a-Kind Wooden "Blood Chit"

This unique two-sided language aid "paddle" was made in a village in China to assist the crew of a C-47 that went down over "The Hump," as the Himalayan Mountains on 28 March 1944.

The crew finally returned to Allied control on 30 June 1944, and the paddle was brought back by one of the crew members named Bob (last name unknown).

One side, shown in the left of the two images, as translated by Dr. Agnes Chan, reads:
"There are four American Air Force members who will be traveling from Guizhou to Chiu [unidentifiable as it is an abbreviation] via Ma-ji [also unidentifiable]. Hope the village chief or Ma-ji will send twenty villagers as escorts. Bring their own food. Compensation will be paid out at a later date. Be sure to follow these directions. To: Village Chief at Ma-ji."

The translation confirms the information in a letter that was acquired along with the paddle regarding its use, what the message was, and naming the crew member as "Bob."

The other side of the paddle, shown in the right-hand image, reads: "29 April 1944."

The paddle was sent by a runner ahead of the crew to Ma-ji as they were being escorted by Chinese villagers from the previous village. It has four large notches representing the number of crew members to be helped, and twenty small notches representing the number of people requested from Ma-ji to help the crew. A portion of the paddle near the top that is broken off is represented by dots in the right-hand image so that the four notches for four crew members can be easily seen.

When we think of theater-made blood chits what usually comes to mind are the beautifully crafted textiles. We can now add to this mental image a simple wooden paddle that contains the requisite characteristics of a blood chit: information about who the foreigners are, what they need, and a promise of compensation for those providing assistance.

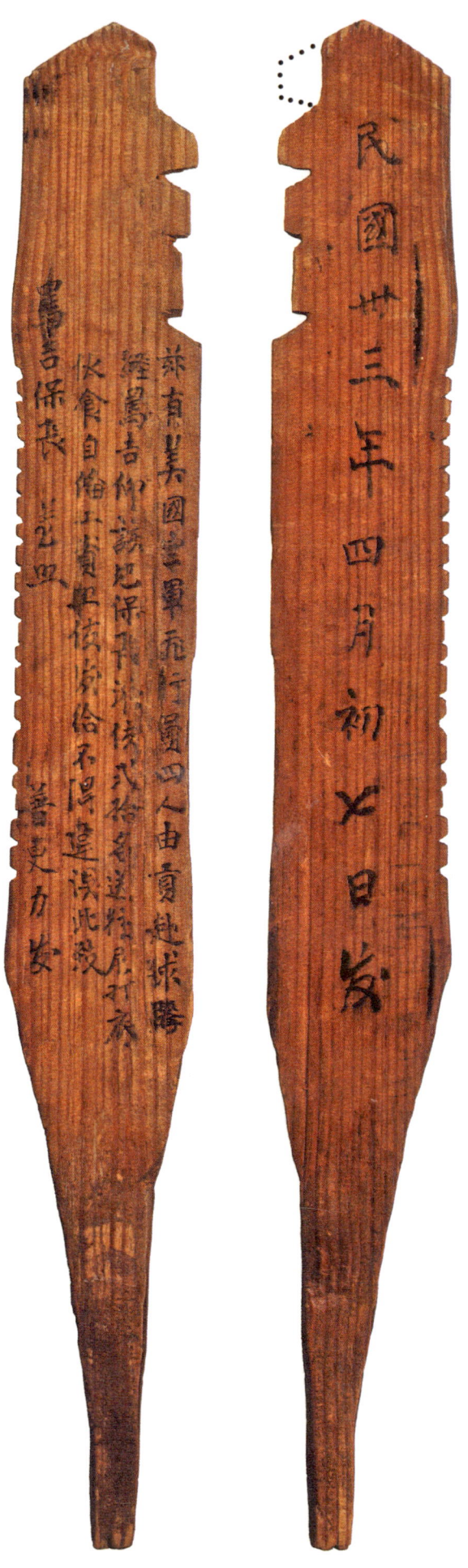

26

Phrase Cards

Phrase Cards were the primary language aid for evaders in Europe to communicate. Perhaps because the likelihood of finding someone who could speak English was fairly good in European countries, phrase cards were not extremely detailed or thorough. Early cards were in four languages and were issued in slipcovers. As operations spread to more countries, a greater number of languages were added to the cards and the use of slipcovers was abandoned.

  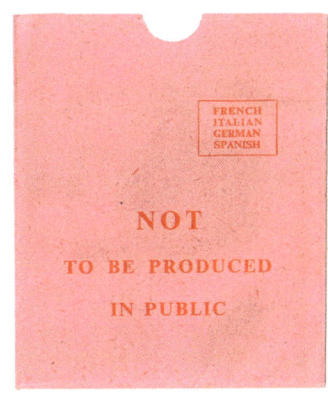 

Phrase card and slipcover in French, Dutch, German, Spanish.   Phrase card and slipcover in French, Italian, German, Spanish.

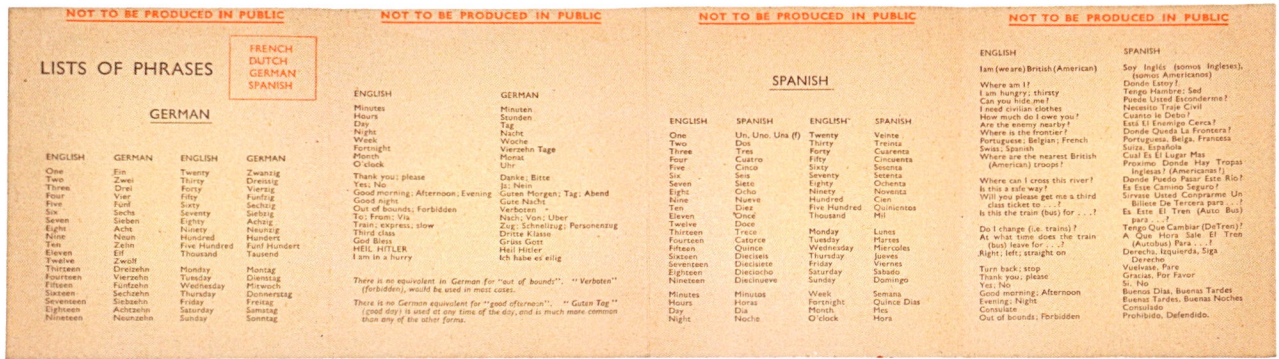

One side of an unfolded phrase card in German and Spanish. The reverse is in French and Dutch.

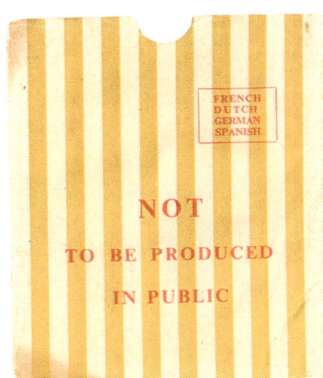  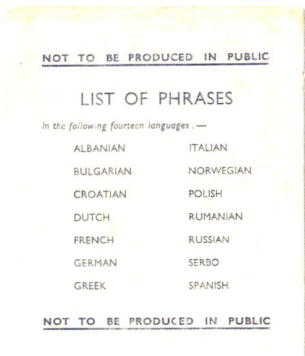 

Left: Phrase card in slipcover in French, Dutch, German and Spanish.
Center: Phrase card without slipcover in 14-languages listed on the front of the card.
Right: Phrase card without slipcover in 14-languages not listed on the card.

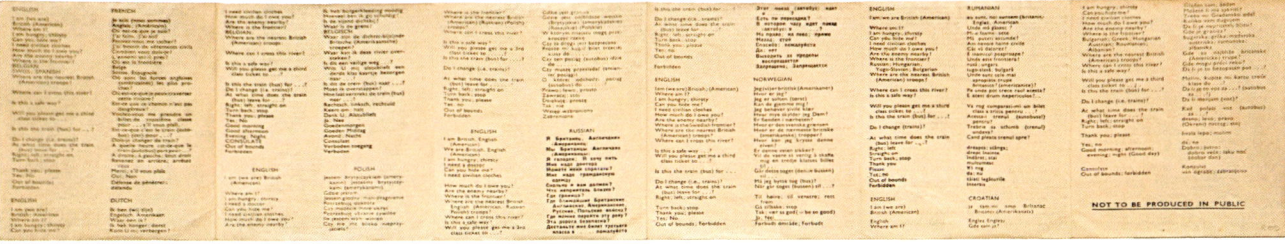

One side of the 14-language phrase card that is shown above right, unfolded.

27

A portion of a 14-language phrase card showing the type of phrases that were included.

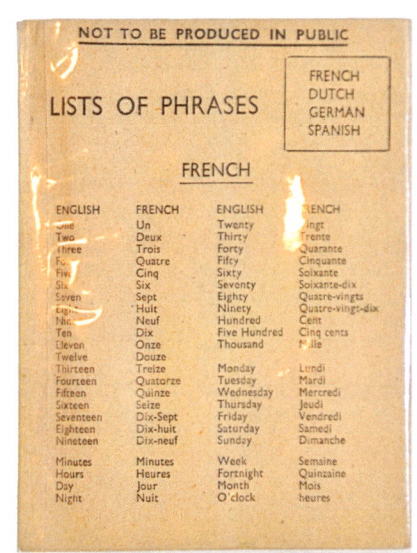

Phrase card enclosed in a cellophane sleeve.

Phrase card printed on watermarked Aerogramme paper.

Map sheets A/B and R1/R2, also printed on Aerogramme paper.

Pointie Talkies

Pointie Talkies became the communication aid of choice in Asia because blood chits, while they could introduce an evader to the locals, did not facilitate detailed conversations. The books were designed so that an airman could point to a statement or question and a local person could point to an answer or response. The trick was finding someone who could read. At first the booklets were produced in one language only, but it was soon found useful to include more languages. Although most of the title pages show the flag of the Kuomintang government of China, some of these booklets contain as many as 8 language sections. Though most Pointie Talkies were in Asian languages, the final U.S. pointie talkie was written in Russian but came too late for use during the war. "Pointie Talkie," like "Walkie Talkie," was simply an easily-remembered name for a useful tool.

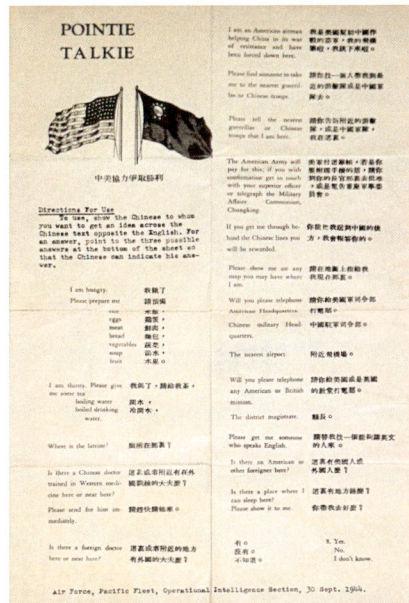
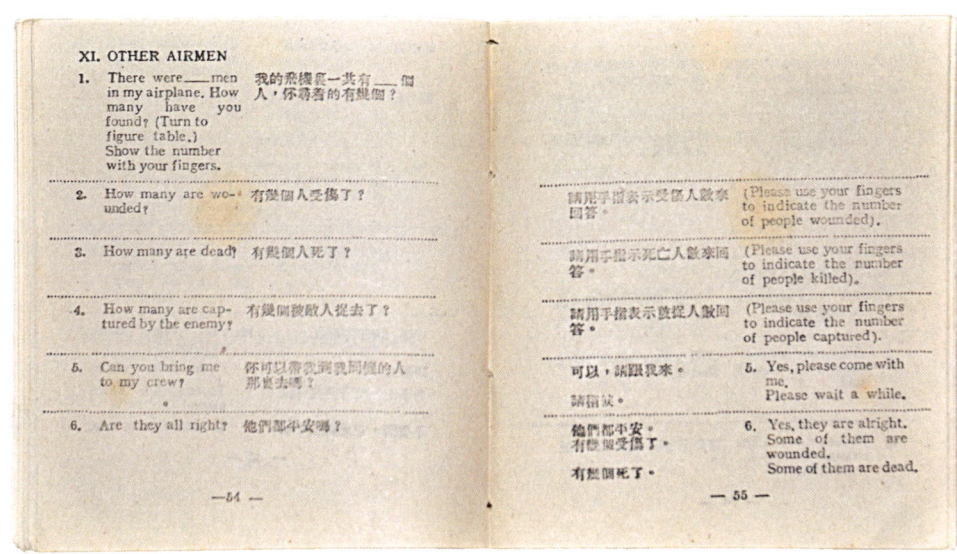

Left: The simplest Pointie Talkie, a single sheet of paper.

Above: Sample pages from a multi-language Pointie Talkie.

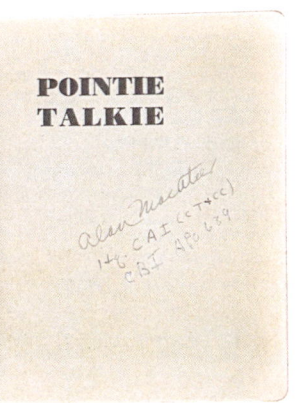

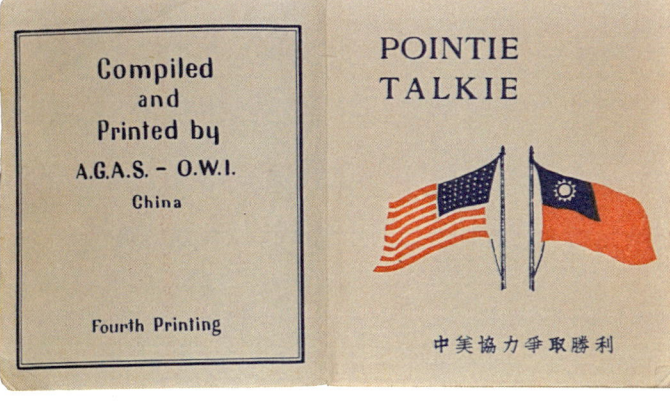
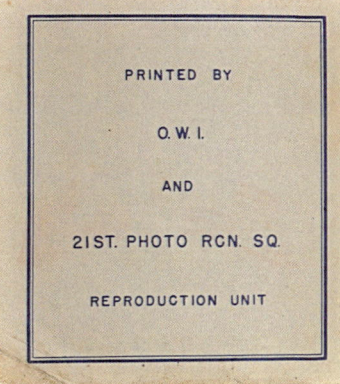
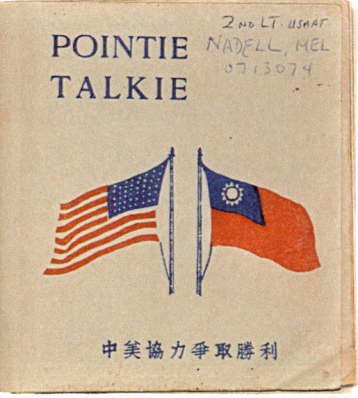

Above: Title pages of four Pointie Talkies.

 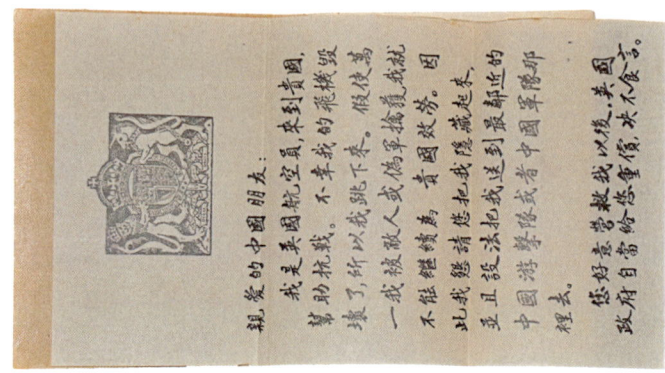

Left: This pointie talkie features a Union Jack with the Nationalist Chinese flag.
Right: Attached to the inside cover is a notice in Chinese beneath the Royal Arms.

 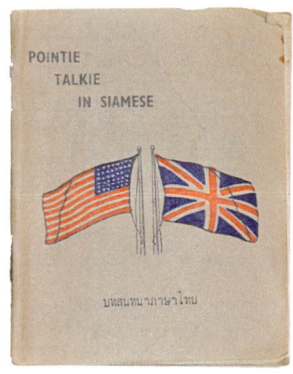 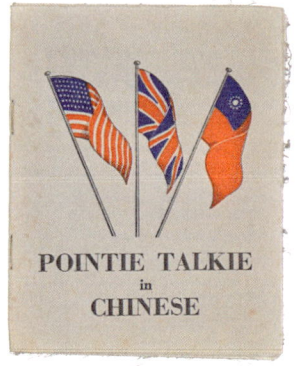

Three single-language Pointie Talkies in Asian languages. The one in Chinese is printed on rayon-acetate.

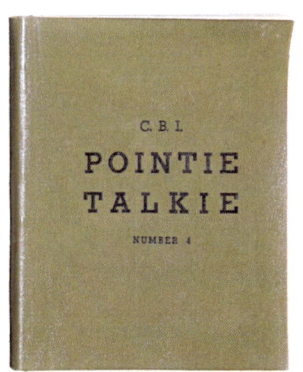 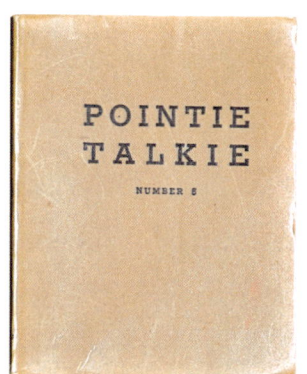 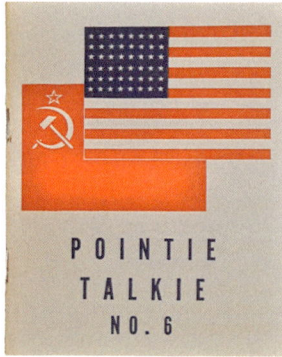

The final three official American Pointie Talkies. Nos. 4 and 5 were for use in Asia, No. 6 was for use when meeting Russian troops in Europe, but was printed too late for actual use in the field.

Left: This small booklet is a pictorial Pointie Talkie for use when encountering people who could not read, a common enough situation. The identical graphics also appear at the end of Pointie Talkie No. 5, shown above.

Aerial Leaflets

While propaganda leaflets dropped from the air were not strictly considered E&E aids, they were extremely important in preparing local populations for the unexpected arrival of an airman from the sky. Most were two-sided and written in propaganda jargon, and some used local proverbs as titles for the leaflet. Many show an airman pointing to a blood chit or flag sewn inside their jacket, and most urge natives to learn to recognize insignia, such as aircraft markings, flags and patches, as belonging to the Allies.

Left: Chinese leaflet front "Plant melons and harvest melons, plant peas and harvest peas," with airman showing his blood chit.
Center: Front of another "Plant melons ..." Chinese leaflet, with stamp cancelled aboard USS Marvin H. McIntyre as a souvenir.
Right: The inside pages of a folded Thai leaflet.

Left: Front of Chinese leaflet, "A good deed has its reward, so has a bad deed."
Top right: Front of "Airman's Picture Pointie" showing airman coming down, being hidden, fed, and disguised.
Bottom right: Back of Chinese leaflet, showing flyer being returned to friendly forces, and flying against the enemy once again.

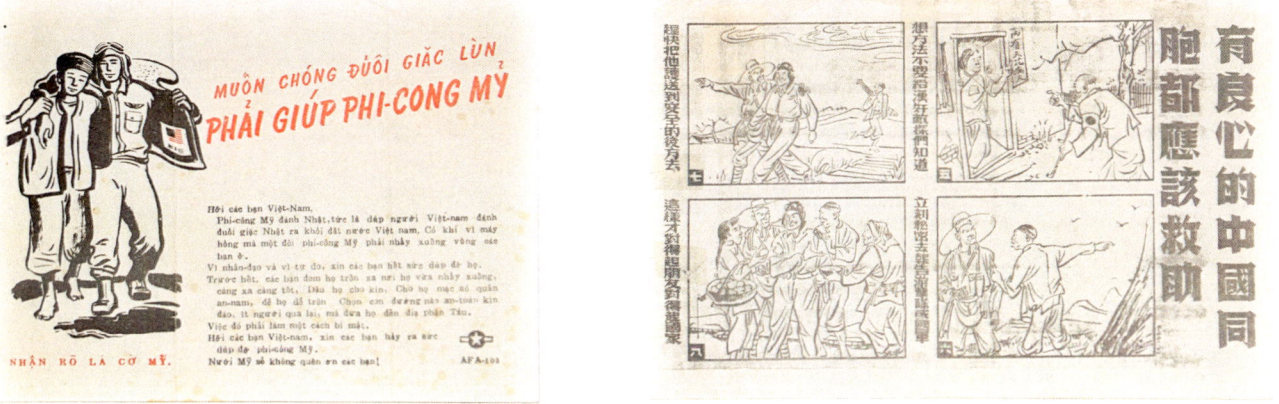

Left: Leaflet in Annamese (Vietnamese) for use in French Indochina. The other side of the leaflet is in French.
Right: Back of a pictorial leaflet in Chinese. Panels are read from top to bottom, right to left.

The inside pages of a folded leaflet in Burmese.

Left: Front of a folded leaflet for Siam.
Center: Front of a folded leaflet for Burma.
Right: Front of a Chinese leaflet, "Amerians will never forget the people who helped them."

Left: Front of a folded leaflet in Chinese.
Center: Front of a leaflet in Annamese (Vietnamese).
Right: Front of a leaflet in Chinese, showing one of China's ethnic minorities aiding a downed American flyer.

Evasion Maps

A compass and a map of the area where a downed flyer might find himself were vital to his evasion of enemy forces. Pre-capture maps were printed on cloth because of its durability, and were included in evasion purses designed for specific areas. This exhibit is designed to illustrate the great variety of mapmakers and the types of maps that were produced, as well as the areas that were covered by them. British maps were printed on silk or on artifical silk (Tenasco), maps from India on silk, Australian maps on silk, and American maps on balloon cloth (Egyptian cotton) or rayon-acetate (Cupramonium).

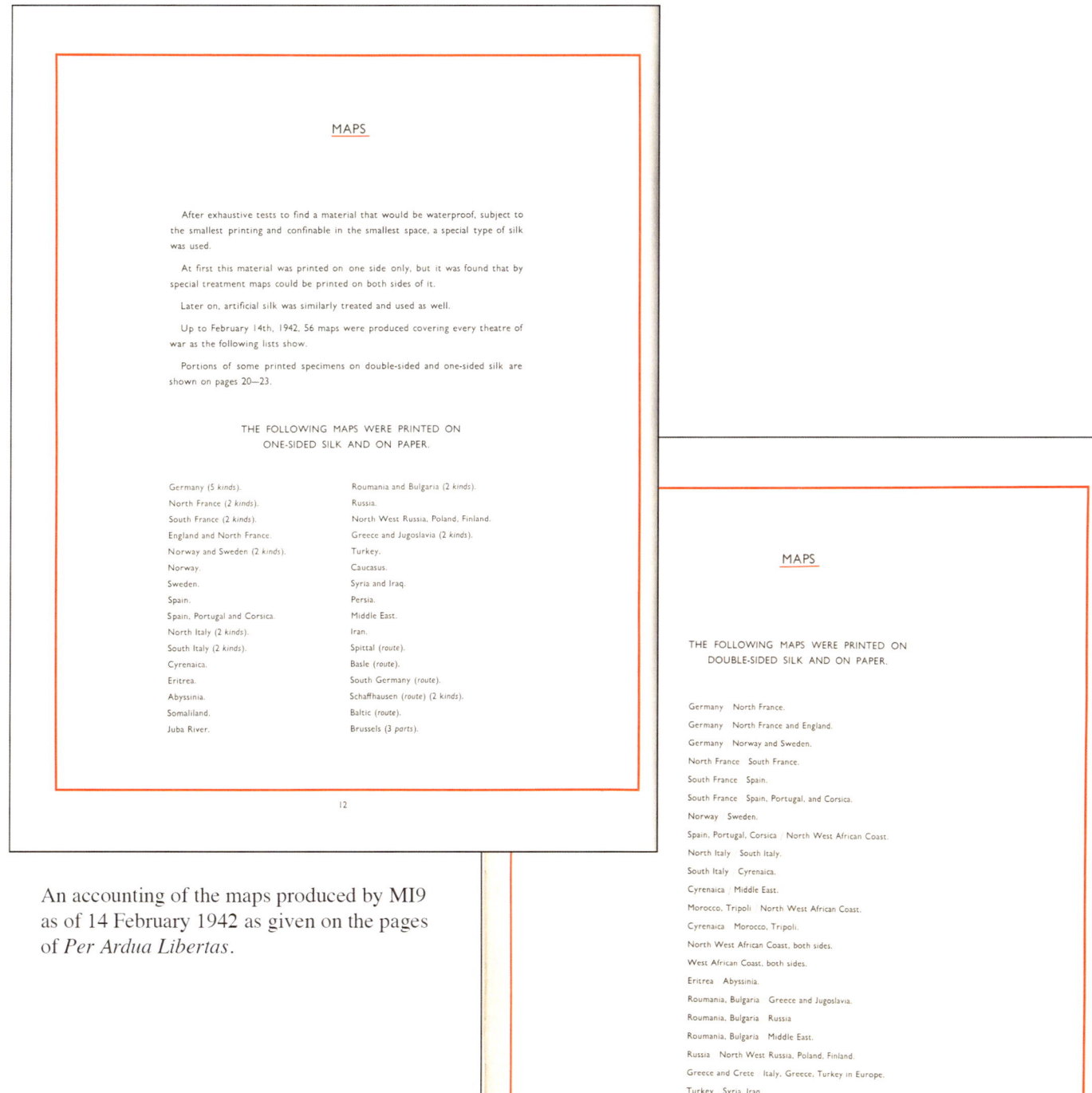

An accounting of the maps produced by MI9 as of 14 February 1942 as given on the pages of *Per Ardua Libertas*.

Left: People tend to forget that the Republic of Ireland maintained neutrality during the war and interned any Allied flyers that landed within its borders. This British two-sided map on artificial silk allowed flyers to evade capture and make their way to Northern Ireland.

Left: This copy of a Michellin road map of West Africa printed on balloon cloth is the first American cloth map of the war.

Below: Detail of a portion of the cloth "Road Map of West Africa."

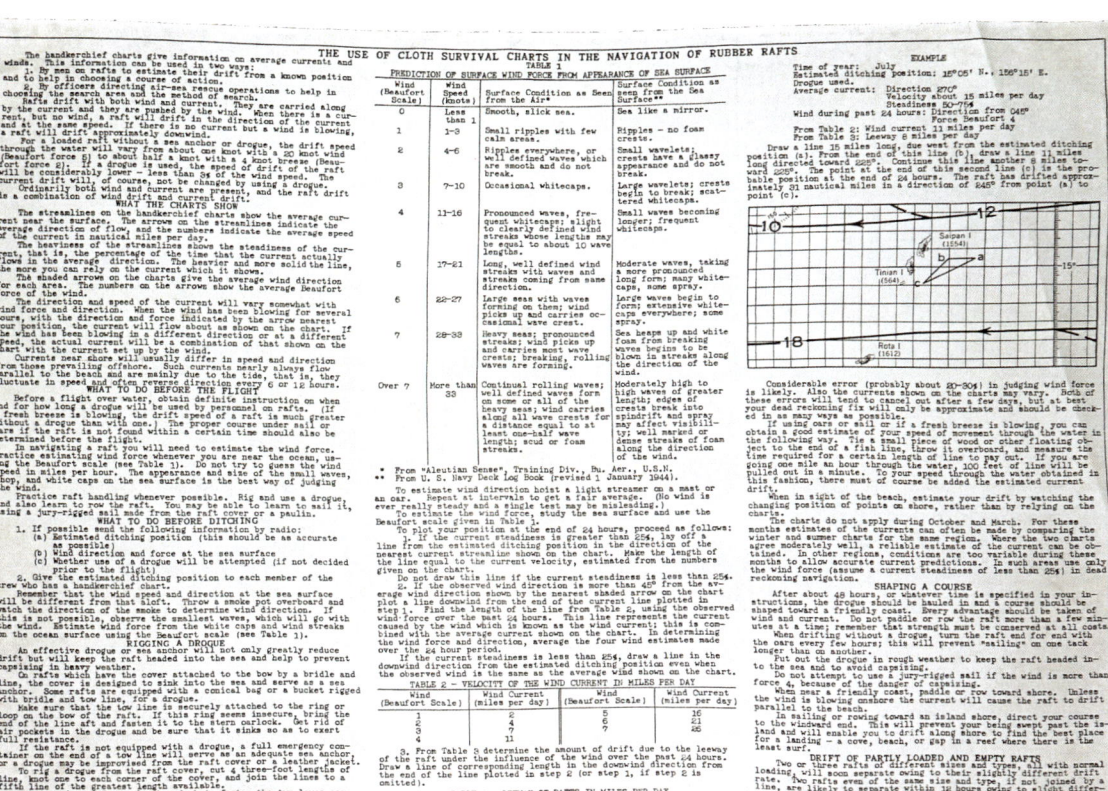

The American Office of Naval Intelligence (ONI) produced a series of cloth drift charts of the Pacific Ocean. Shown here is the cover sheet explaining how to use the charts for navigating rubber rafts.

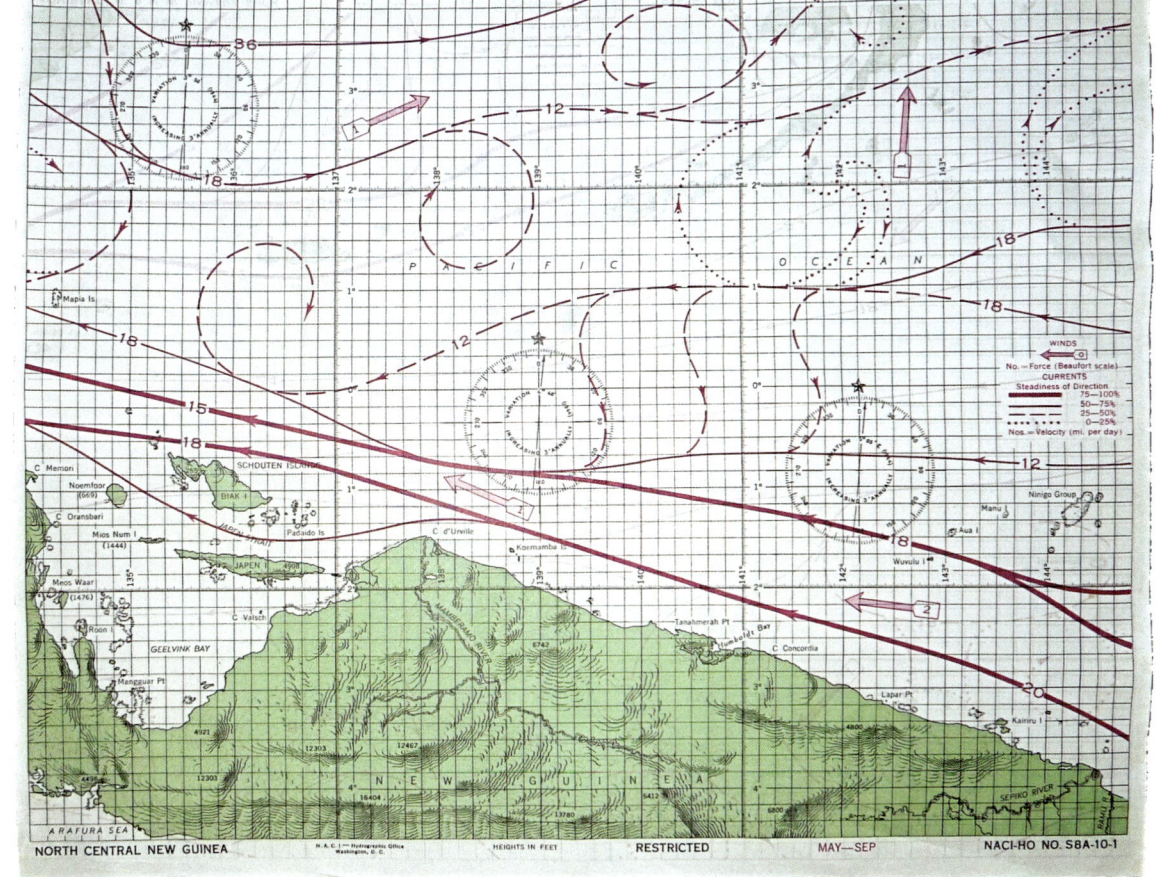

This ONI drift chart of North Central New Guinea shows wind direction and water currents that could be expected from May through September.

Left: This British silk map of portions of eastern Turkey, Georgia, Armenia, Azerbaijan, Syria, Trans-Jordan, Palestine, Iraq and Iran is one of the few specialty sheets that was not a part of a series containing other maps.

Below: Detail of sheet showing map nomenclature.

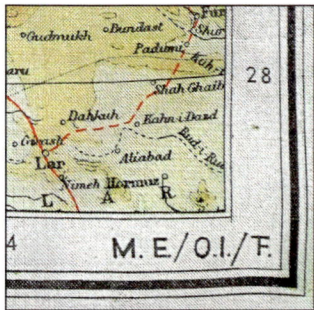

Right: The *Zones of France* map made by Intelligence School 9 (IS9) shows the zones within France that were created by Germany. Often considered a map made for Operation Overlord, the Allied invasion of France, because many sheets are dated March 1944, this example dating from December 1942, reveals it to be an older sheet.

Below: Detail of Zones of France map showing map nomenclature.

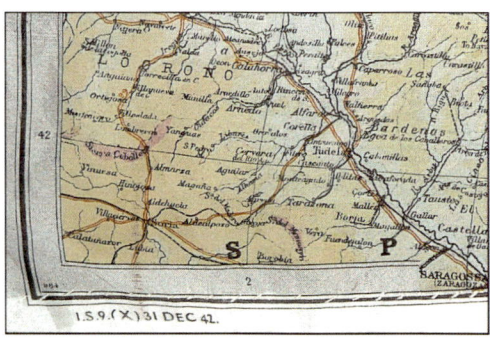

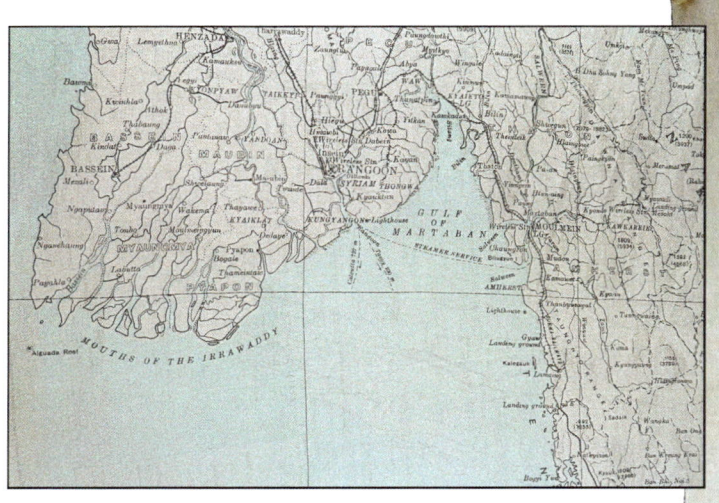

Above: Detail of SOI *Upper Burma and Siam* map.

Right: British Survey of India (SOI) silk map sheet *Lower Burma and Siam*, with blue water. On the reverse is sheet *Upper Burma and Assam*. This map was officially known in Asia as DEM-3.

Above: Detail of a portion of sheet 44F

Left: In 1944 Britain issued a series of artificial silk maps with heat-sealed edges covering parts of Asia. This is sheet 44F. On the reverse is Sheet 44E covering a portion of Sumatra and northern Siam.

Above: Detail of sheet 133.

Right: This American map on rayon-acetate is a copy of the Aeronautical Chart over the Himalayan Mountains from Assam, India, to Kunming, China. In the border are blood chits in languages found along the route.

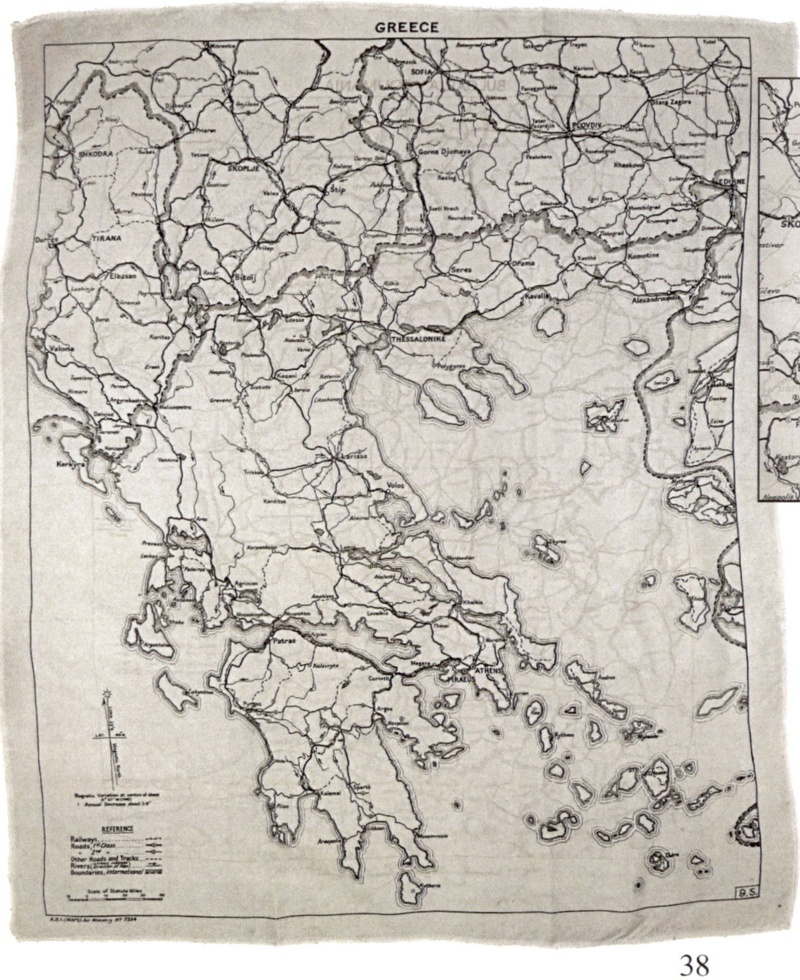

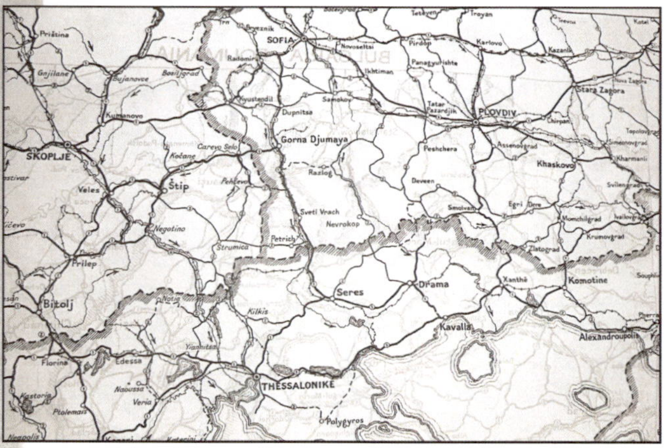

Above: Detail of a portion of Sheet 9S.

Left: Sheet 9S, Greece, is one of a series of British Air Ministry maps of Europe printed on silk. On the reverse of this sheet is Sheet 9T, Bulgaria and Roumania.

Above: Large British map, 1:500,000 Europe (Air) Sheet N.E. 42/14, *Chieti*, on artificial silk. In the upper right is a portion of the coast of Yugoslavia, and at the lower left is a portion of the coast of Italy. On the reverse is Sheet N.E. 42/18, *Shkodra*.

Right: One of a series of British 1:500,000 Europe (Air) maps on silk. Due to their small size (approx. 41 by 33 cm) the single-sided maps are known as "Air Miniatures." This is Sheet L 32/8 *Milan*.

Above: US Sheet 7, *Mediterranean France*, printed on Rayon Acetate, one of only 4 US sheets covering areas of Europe. The reverse side is Sheet 8, *Lyon Torino*.

Left: Britain made a series of maps on artificial silk with heat-sealed edges in 1943, which covered Europe. This is sheet 43H covering the Aegean Sea. On the reverse is Sheet 43G covering the slavic countries of Eastern Europe.

Above: Detail of a portion of the early "Blue Water" map.
Left: One sheet of an early series of British silk maps with blue water covered portions of Italy and North Africa. This sheet covers part of the Tunisia to the west and the south of Tunis.

Below: Two maps, *Millingimbi* and *Darwin*, are printed on this Royal Australian Air Force (RAAF) silk sheet. Only *Darwin* is shown. The arrows on the map point to Air Rescue Dumps established to aid pilots who were downed defending against Japanese attacks. This map was carried by RAAF pilot William Oswald Cable, D.F.C.

Evasion Purses

Airmen were issued small kits called "purses" containing items for evading capture in the event that they were forced down in enemy-controlled territory. Items in kits included maps, a compass, a hacksaw blade, currency, and sometimes language aids. In Europe the purses were designated by the colors of the stripes on the upper left front of the purse, and a white "43" over the stripes indicated that the purse contained the newer 1943 maps. The letters on the front of the purse designated the type of currency they contained. "Maps Only" purses did not contain currency, and some were marked as to the map sheet numbers that they contained. Many purses shown do not contain all of their original contents. Items noted * were excluded from the exhibition due to space constraints but are shown here as a special "Virtual Frazier" feature. Evasion purses are categorized as pre-capture aids.

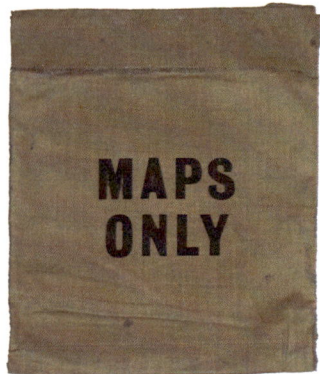

Left: Maps Only Purse, with contents in original unopened inner pouch, and phrase card stapled to pouch.
Right: Maps Only Purses, containing the map sheets stamped on them. Maps would be of the 1943 series.

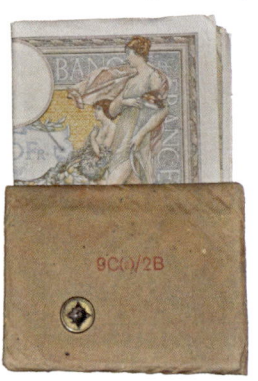

Left: Early, sun-bleached, Red Purse with map sealed in paper, compass, and French currency.
Right: Mark II Red Purse with contents in original inner pouch.

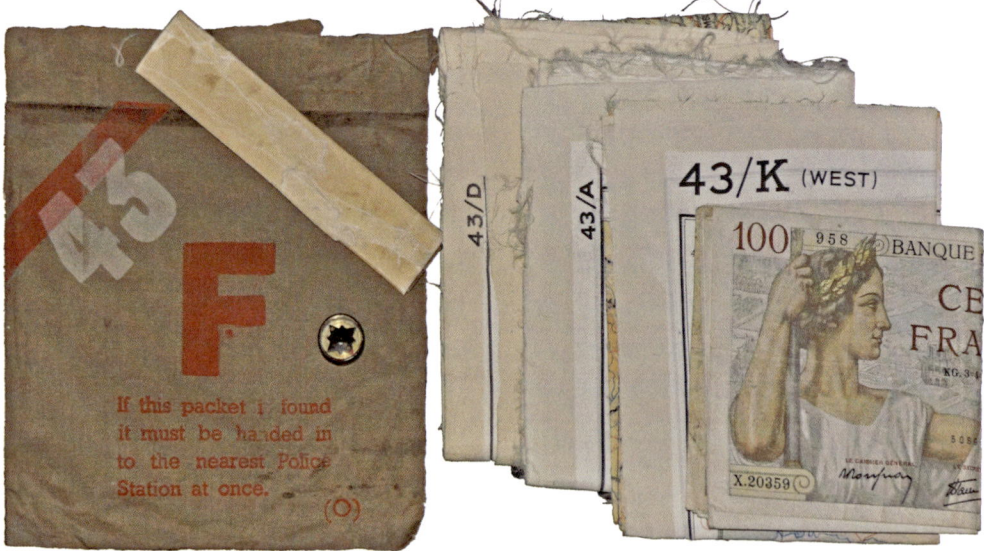

Mark III Red 43 Purse with contents: hacksaw blade wrapped in paper, compass three maps, and French currency. Note the white "43" over the red stripe, indicating that the maps in the purse are from the 1943 series.

Green/Blue Purse with contents: hacksaw, compass, five maps of Europe and North Africa, and Italian and French currency.

Left: Red/Green Purse.
Center: Mauve Purse with contents, including saw encased in rubber and Norwegian currency.
Right: US Purse.*

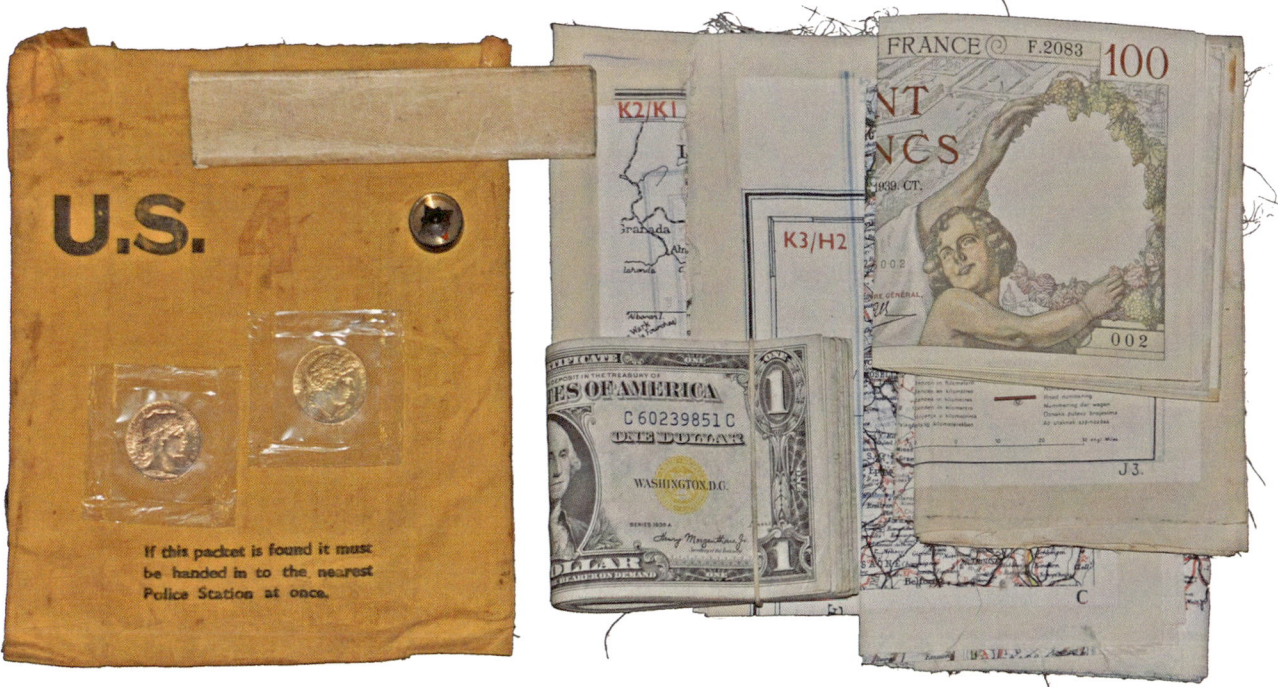

US 4 Purse with contents, including French currency, American yellow-seal currency, and French gold coins.

Lady Be Good crash site
USAF Photo (Public Domain)

Above is all that remains of a purse that was recovered from the B-24 *Lady Be Good*, which went missing on a mission in 1943. It shows the effects of being in the Libyan desert for 25-years. It was a gift from Walter Willet IV, and originally belonged to his friend Jim Walker, the McDonnell-Douglas engineer who initiated the 1968 expedition to the crash site. Given the mission of *Lady Be Good* when she went down and the Italian currency, the purse was likely a Red Green or a Green/Blue Purse.

Left: White purse, covering most of Europe. This purse was sewn shut in-theater, probably as a repair after the glue failed.
Center: Mark II 43 Yellow Purse* that belonged to Intelligence Officer Schramm, who collected various examples.
Right: This Yellow 43 + Purse (note the stamped "+") was carried by F/Lt G. S. Irving, who flew night fighters with 125 Squadron, RAF. The contents are in the original inner pouch. It contains French, Belgian, and Dutch currency.

Left: This American version of a purse for use in North Africa consists of a cloth pouch containing the balloon cloth Road Map of West Africa, and a booklet, with cultural information and language aids.

 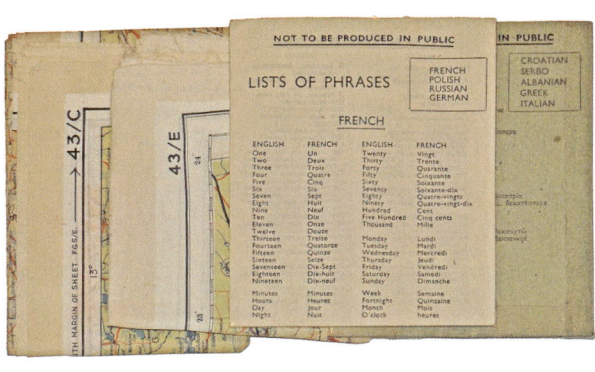 

Left: CMF Pack containing two phrase cards in cellophane, compass, and hacksaw in cellophane. It is assumed from the languages on the phrase cards that there should be another map, 43G/43H, in the purse covering Eastern Europe.
Right: Another CMF Pack*, for Central Mediterranean Forces, with different printing on the cover.

Left: Black/Mauve Purse and contents: hacksaw in paper, compass, maps, and Danish currency.
Right: Just a few of the types of hacksaw blades that were enclosed in purses.*

Money purse for use in China. Inside the outer green cloth pouch is a waterproof envelope also stamped "C" (faintly, just above where the envelope is cut) containing 4900 Yuan in consecutively numbered 100 Yuan notes. MIS-X documents specify 5000 Yuan.

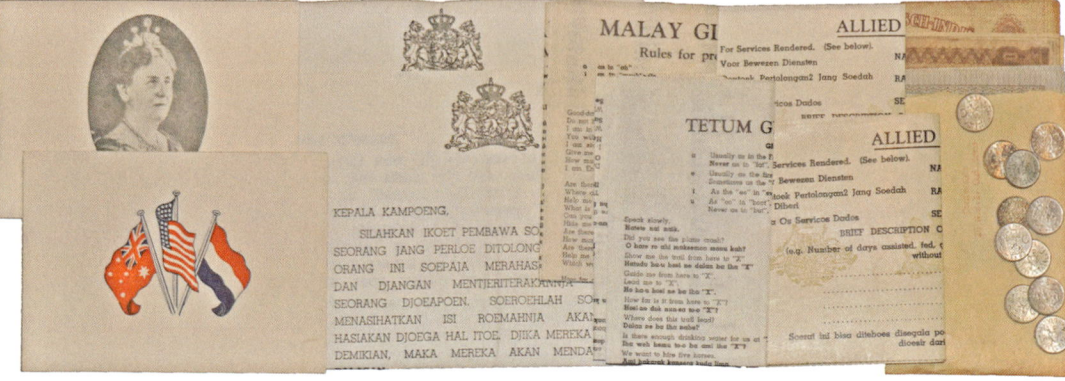

Purse for Netherlands East Indies: leatherette wallet containing folded card blood chits in Malay for NEI and in Tetum for Portuguese Timor, 2 paper letters to village chieftains in Malay, Malay and Tetum Glossaries on onionskin paper, six promissory notes, and an envelope containing 25 Guilders in NEI currency and silver coin.

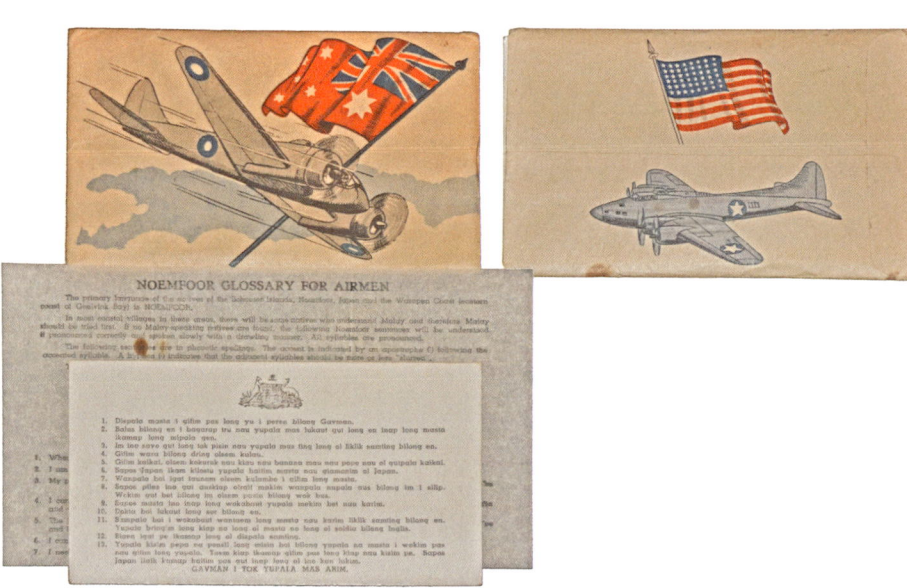

Left: Paper envelope with essentially the same NEI contents as the leatherette wallet shown above it.*
Right: Paper envelope containing a Pidgen English blood chit on cardstock and a Noemfoor Glossary on onionskin paper, for use in New Guinea. The back of the envelope is shown to the right. This was issued to a S/Sgt Nordin.

Unmarked purse evidently for use in Burma containing compass on lanyard, hacksaw encased in rubber, silk blood chit, two maps, paper pointie talkie, currency and silver coins.

Unmarked purse for use in Malaya. Inside waterproof roll-up cloth pouch are a compass encased in rubber, silk blood chit, rayon Malay language booklet, one cloth map, paper Malay pointie talkie booklet, rayon Chinese pointie talkie, rayon survival booklet, and Straits Dollars.

 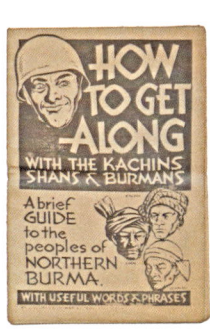 

Left: Waterproof pouch containing a Survey of India map of Burma dyed orange, presumably to be used as a signal panel, and a paper leaflet with cultural information and useful phrases.
Right: Roll-up pouch containing a compass, blood chits, and maps of China and Burma. The CBI patch was included in some kits because the Chinese recognized this is an American symbol. Both sides of the pouch are shown.*

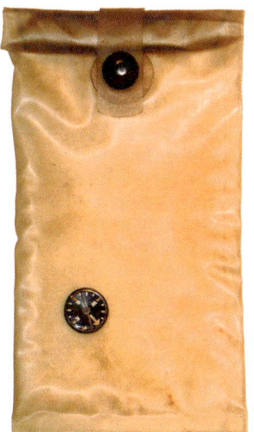  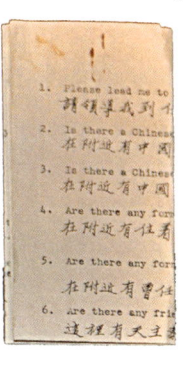 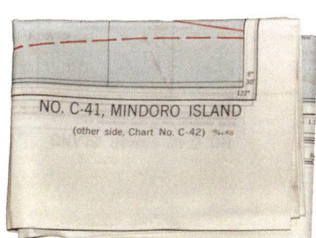
 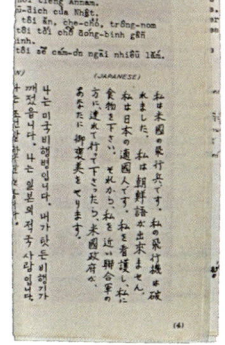  

From the serial number on the Chinese blood chit, this is evidently a kit used by the 25th Photo Reconaissance Squadron in the Pacific Theater. Four of the five map sheets (two 2-sided maps and one 1-sided map) are of Philippine Islands, the fifth is of Southwest China. Pilots were instructed that they could fly to China if they were unable to ditch in a safe area, hence the numerous aids for use in China in this kit, including a paper pointie talkie and paper leaflet.

Personal Aids Kits

Small kits containing food and medicine were devised by various E&E agencies and issued to aircrew. The first were created by Christopher Clayton Hutton of Britain's MI-9, and later boxes were prepared by the armed services. Hutton called his creations "Ration Boxes," but later military correspondence refers to them as "Aids Boxes." American kits were referred to as "Personal Aids" Kits and "Emergency Kits," and the letter "E" in the names of American kits stands for "Emergency." They are sometimes just referred to as Survival Kits. There were many types, from small personal kits to large kits in vests and those that fit into aircraft seat cushions. This exhibit contains only the small personal kits carried by airmen. Items noted * were excluded from the exhibition due to space constraints but are shown here as a special "Virtual Frazier" feature. Kits shown are pre-capture aids.

British Aids Box, apparently a variation of Ration Box 2 with only the inner box, Top of box reveals a tube of cream, matches, Horlicks tablets, chocolate bar, halazone, and a stimulant. Bottom of box reveals a compass and rubber water bottle.

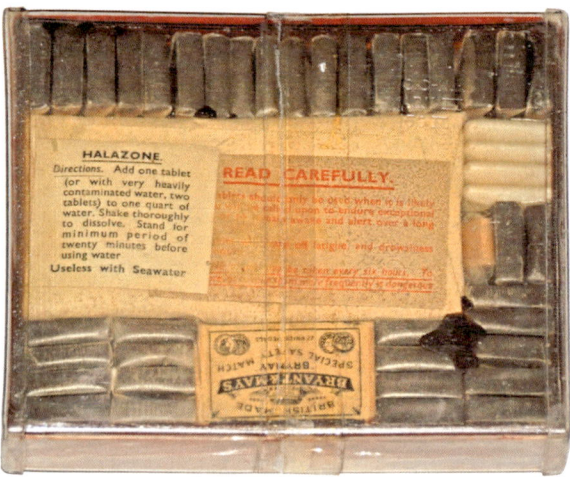 

British Aids Box. Top of box reveals Horlicks tablets, matches, peanut bars, Halazone and a stimulant. Bottom of box reveals a compass and rubber water bottle. Embossed into the top of the box is the nomenclature "C.C-V. Mk III. 50M".

This box was curved so that it would better fit into a pocket of the flight suit. A compass is visible on the left hand side.

British Aids Box. Top reveals matches, a sewing kit, gum, Horlicks tablets, tape, barley sugar, and a rolled-up rubber water bottle. Bottom reveals peanut bars, some of the Horlicks tablets, the rubber water bottle, and a date of July 1944.

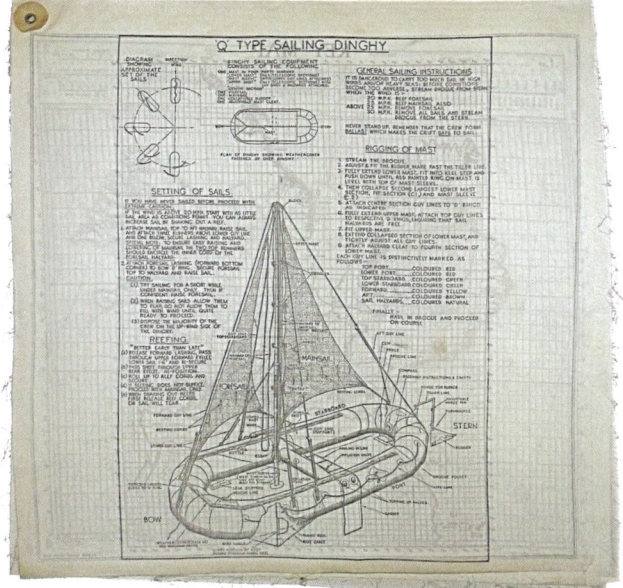 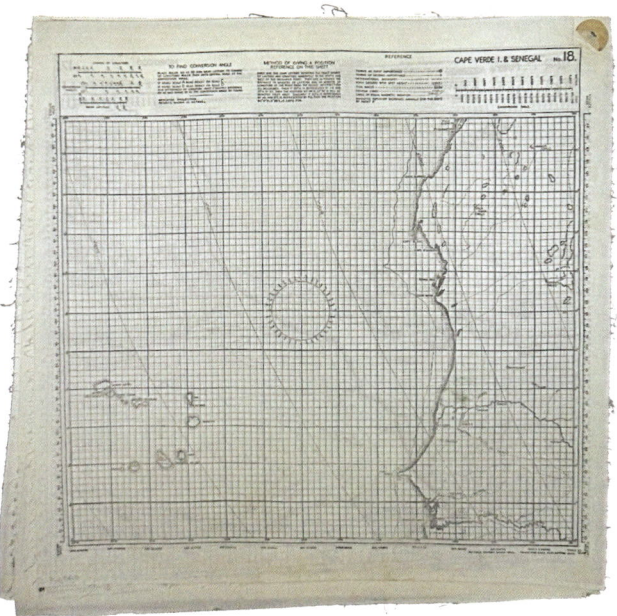

British aids for airmen forced down at sea.
Top: Fishing kit containing hook, lure, sinker, line, and cloth instruction book. Shown closed and opened.
Bottom: Set of 18 cloth charts showing the coastline of the Atlantic Ocean and Mediterranean Sea, from Iceland to Senegal, plus a key map and instructions for sailing the Q Dinghy. Held together with a gromet. Both the front and back sheets of the set are shown.

Above: The E-3 Personal Sustenance Kit was the first American personal aids kit. It contains a match safe with a compass in the top, six lemon and nine malted milk destrose tablets, a packet of instant bouillion, four sticks of gum, adhesive tape, a field ration D-bar, aspirin, a stimulant, and a hacksaw blade. A cloth bag to hold the contents of the kit after it is opened is visible through the bottom of the box.

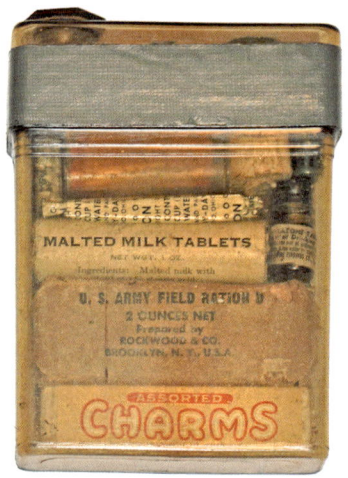 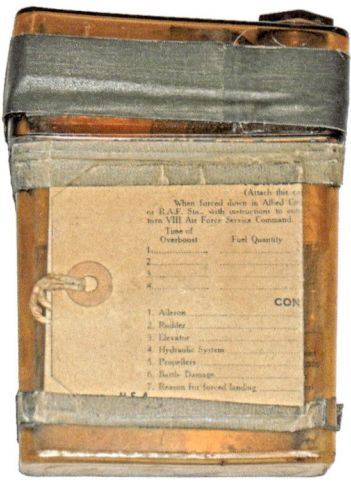 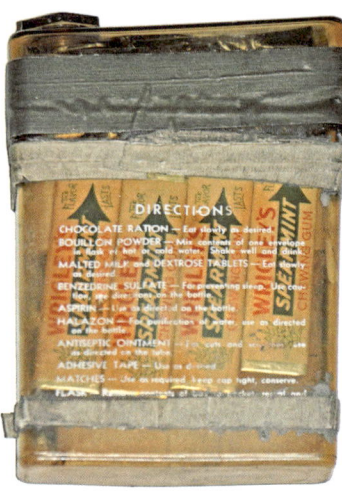

Left: Unknown kit. Survival kit authority Bob Lemacher documented a kit like this, speculating that it was an E-3 "spec revision."
Right: Both sides of a USAAF "Tape-Top" E-3A Kit, with a card for the airman to return if forced down in friendly territory to gather information on the cause of bail out, and the effectiveness of the survival kit. Green tape may appear silver in images.

 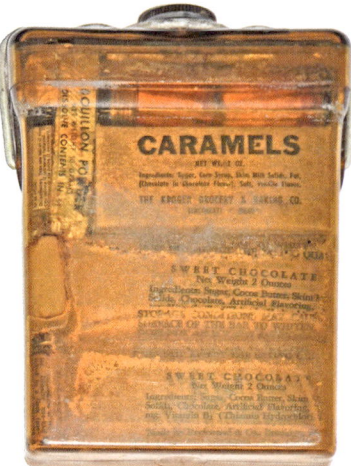 

Left: Image illustrating the difference between "tape-top" kit and "bale top" kit closures.
Right. Both sides of a USAAF "Bale-Top" E-3A Kit.

Left: Both sides of a U.S. Navy Mark I Personal Aids Kit. Similar to the Army Air Force E-3A kit, this kit was customized for naval personnel.

Below: Image illustrating how both containers and the mirror in cardboard fit insidethe canvas pouch.

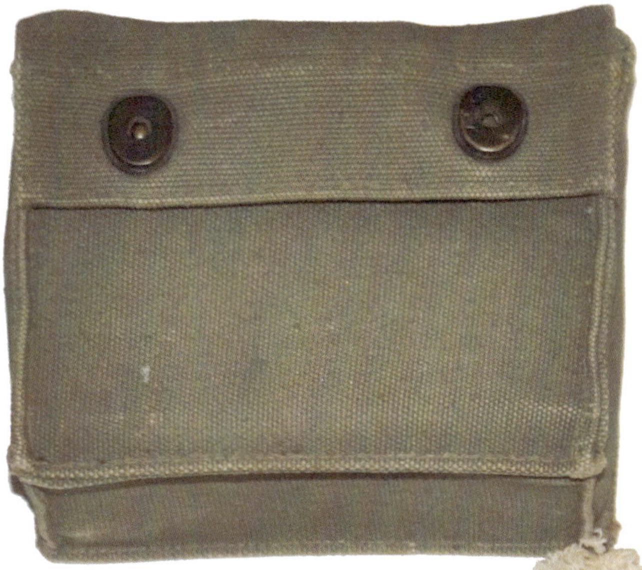

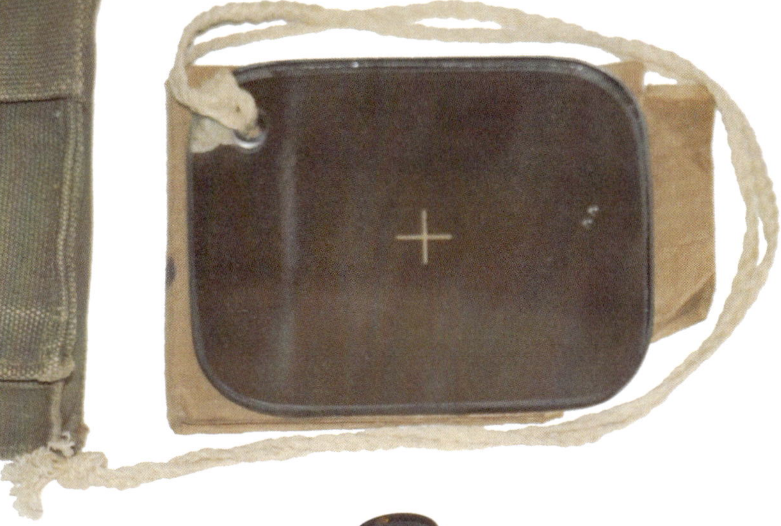

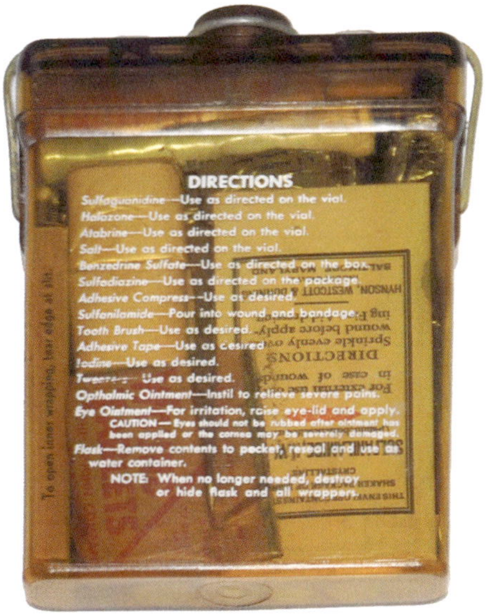

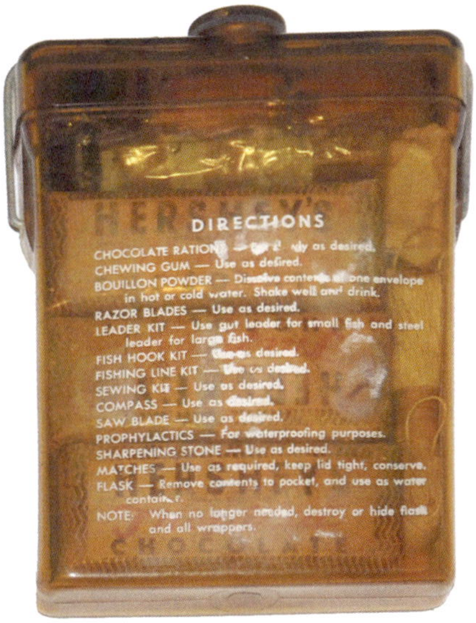

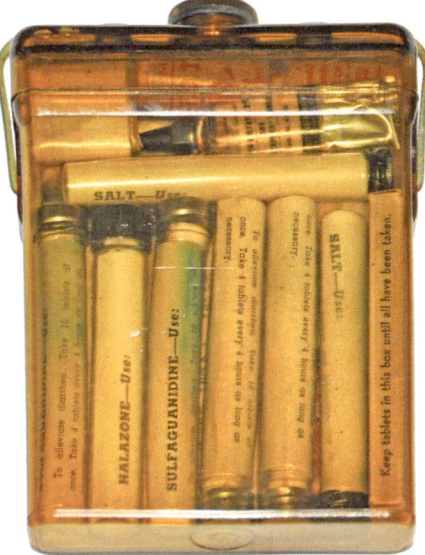

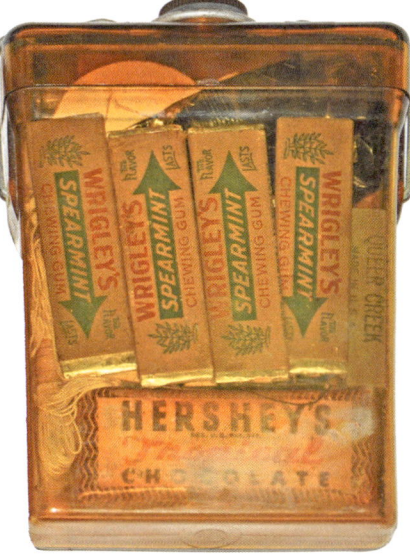

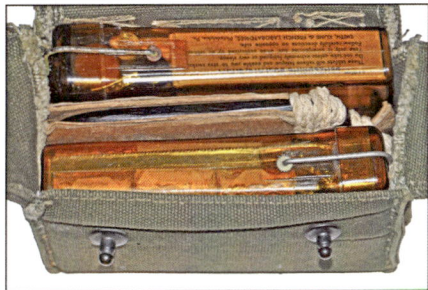

USAAF E-17 Kit. Top left: Canvas pouch. Top right: Signaling mirror with neck lanyard and protective cardboard. Center: The side of the two containers with lists of contents. Bottom left and center: Other side of the two containers.

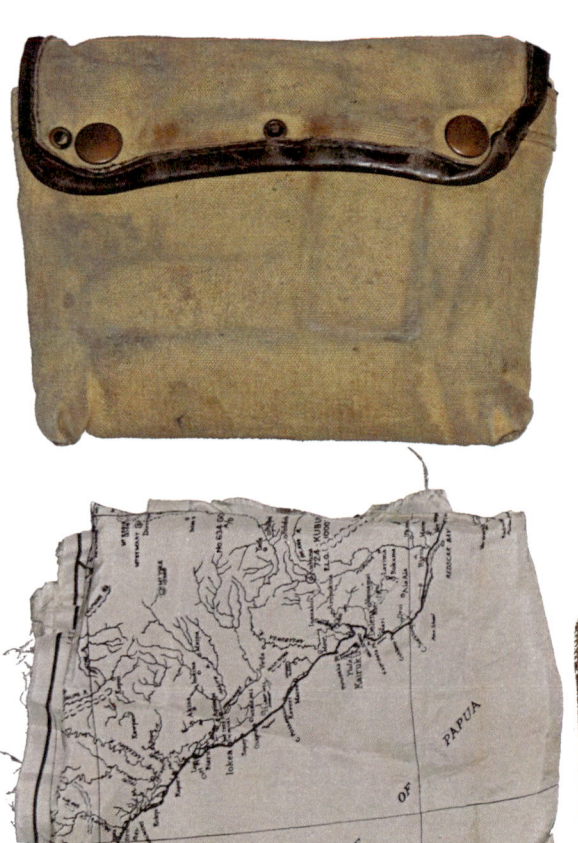
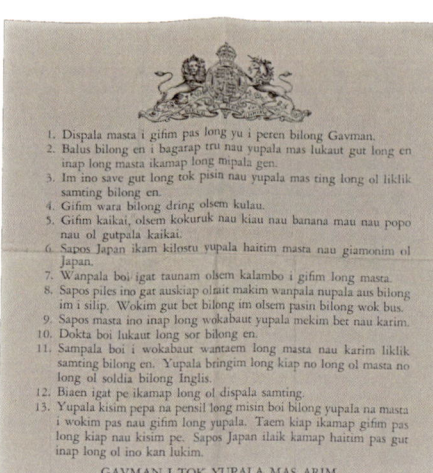

Royal Australian Air Force (RAAF) evasion and survival kit for the South West Pacific Area (SWPA), consisting of a paper blood chit in Pidgin English, survival booklet, silk map, cricket spikes, compass, waterproofed tin of matches, razor blades and safety pins. The razor blades and safety pins were valued by the people of the area and could be given as rewards for assistance. Cricket spikes are cleats that screw into the soles of boots to give traction in the mud, and a spanner for attaching them is included.

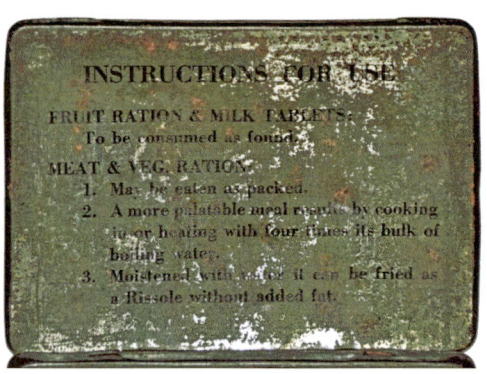
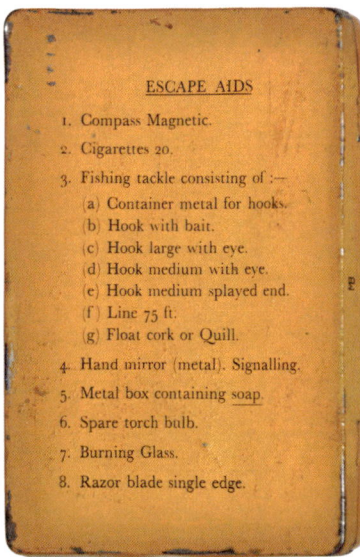
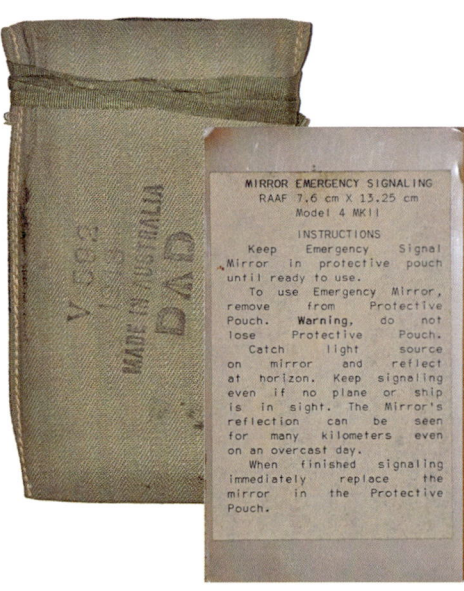

Top left: Australian ration box made from a cigarette tin. Bottom left: Instructions on how to prepare rations are given inside lid of ration box.

Center: "Escape Aids" box containing many survival items made from a cigarette tin, thought to be Australian as it was collected with the ration box.

Right: Signaling mirror in cloth pouch. Instructions on back of mirror are shown.

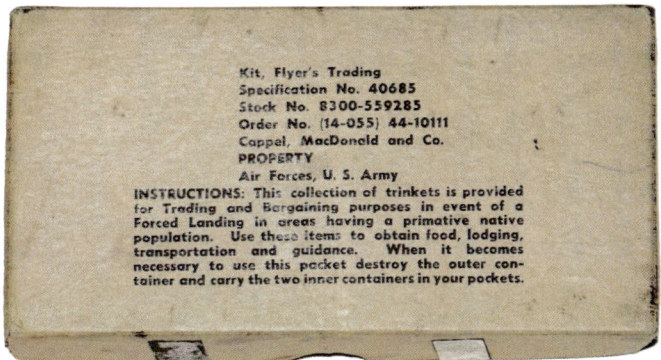 

Left: The USAAF Flyer's trading kit contains trinkets, twist tobacco, and other items valued by peoples of the Pacific.
Right: Burning glasses were issued to flyers in the Pacific, and sometimes included in the roll-up kits with maps and blood chits.*

  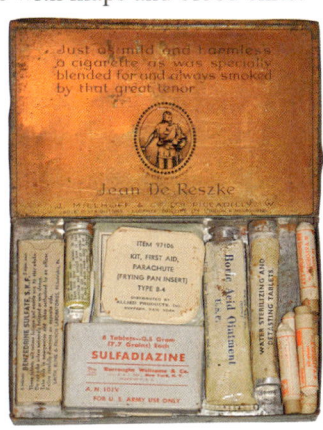

Burning glass in envelope with instructions.*

This cigarette tin carried by Sgt. Pilot Ron Soper of 34 Squadron in Burma contains various first aid items from other kits. The theater-made kit is genuine and came with a letter from the pilot.*

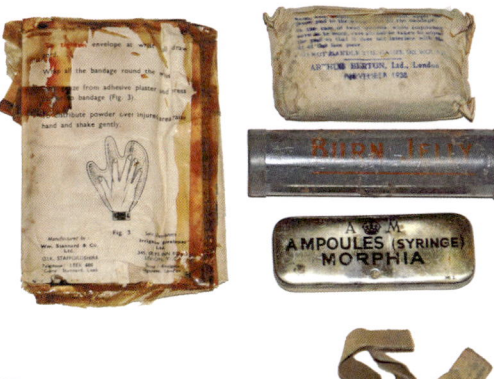

 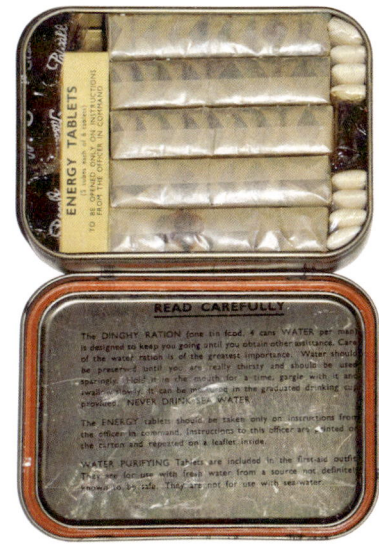

Left: RAF air crew first aid kit, basically a burn kit. The container is shown at the bottom, contents at the top (the two safety pins in the kit are now holding the cover closed).
Center: RAF tropical first aid kit in a tin, The inside of the lid lists contents.
Right: British emergency flying rations were not intended for survival purposes, but would have been available to downed flyers if they had not been consumed druing flight.

   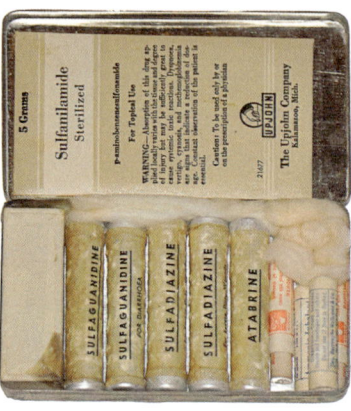

Left: Asiatic Kit made in-theater from parts of the E-17 Kit, with additional items added. The list of contents was scraped off of the E-17 flask and a paper list of contents inserted.

Right: Unhappy with the kits issued by the government, John L. Cella, Escape and Evasion and Search and Rescue Officer of the Twentieth Bomber Command, had this first aid kit made in India and issued it to crews. The cardboard box on the left side contained a morphene syrette. A gift of John L. Cella.*

In addition to kits and aids, air crews were trained in survival and a number of booklets on the subject were provided. Some of the booklets are shown below.

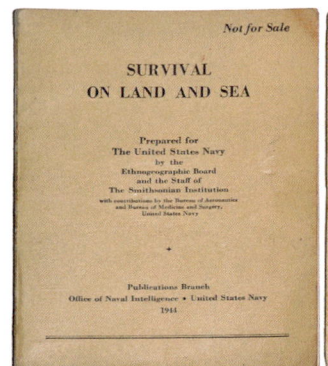 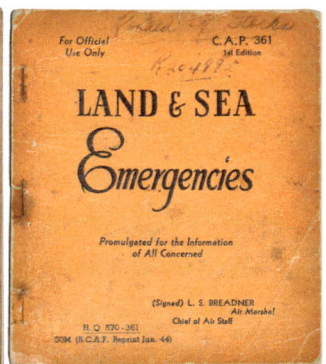  

   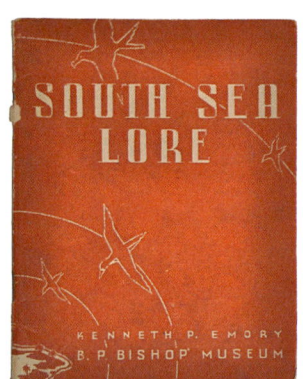

Bottom four booklets courtesy of Virtual Frazier*

54

Escape Aids - A British Perspective

These images are only a few of many pages from *Per Ardua Libertas*, and provide an inside view of Escape Aids as seen by MI-9, the British agency that designed and procured them. All of the aids shown in these pages were in production by February 1942. Escape Aids are considered *post*-capture items.

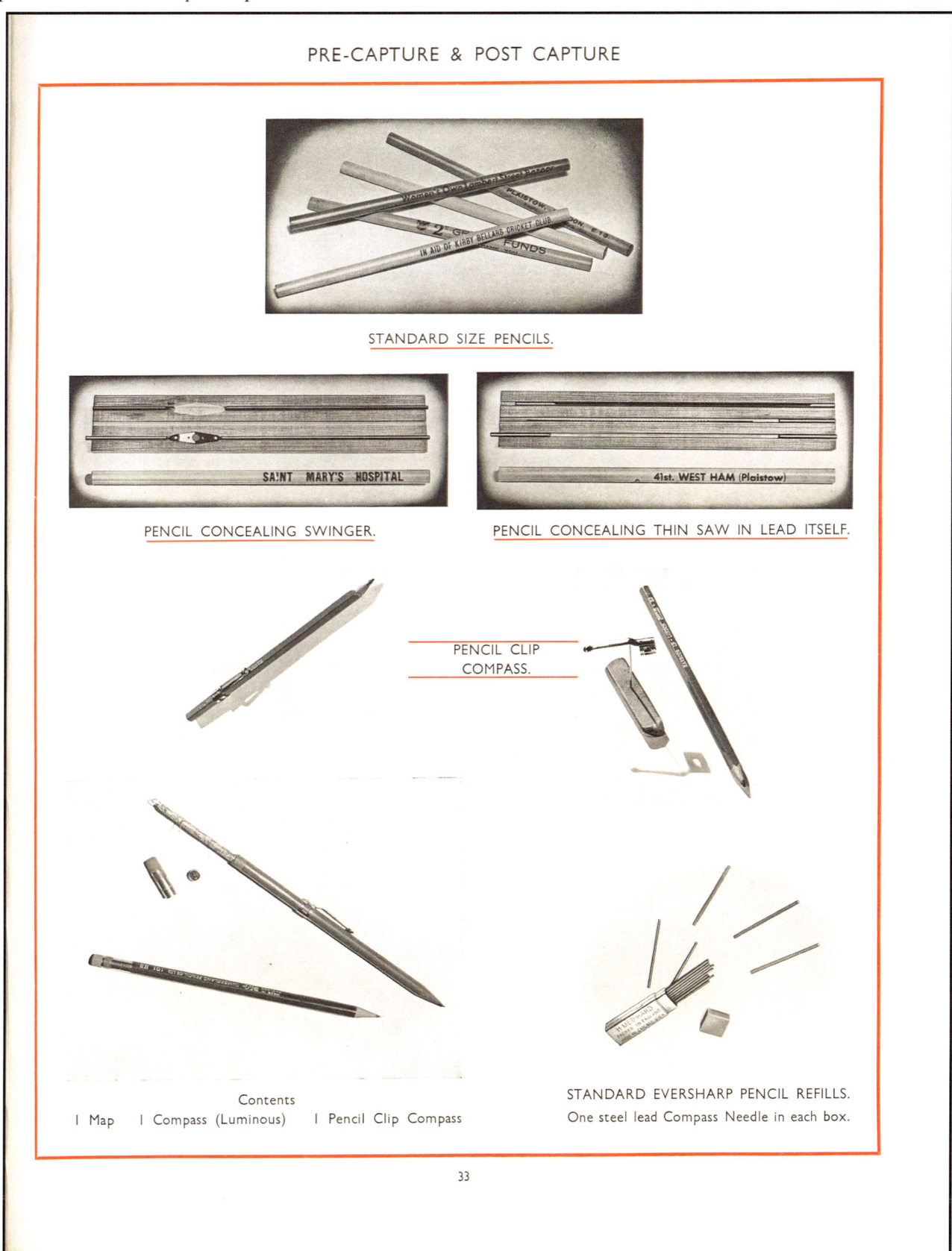

POST CAPTURE

GAMES CARRIERS AND THEIR CONTENTS.
(Maps and various escape aids)

SMALL CHESS SET.

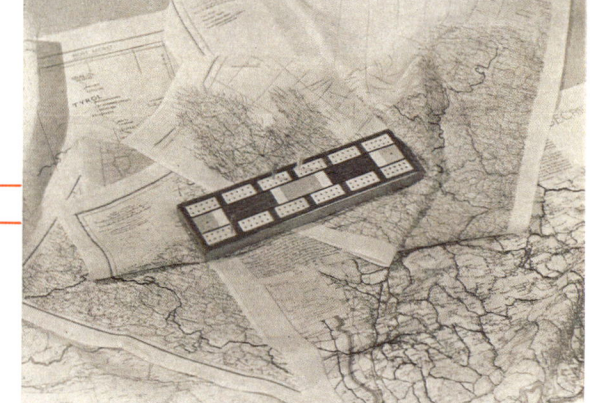

CRIBBAGE BOARD.

SQUASH RACKET.

POST CAPTURE

GAMES CARRIERS AND THEIR CONTENTS.
(Maps and various escape aids)

MEDIUM CHESS SET.

BACKGAMMON SET.

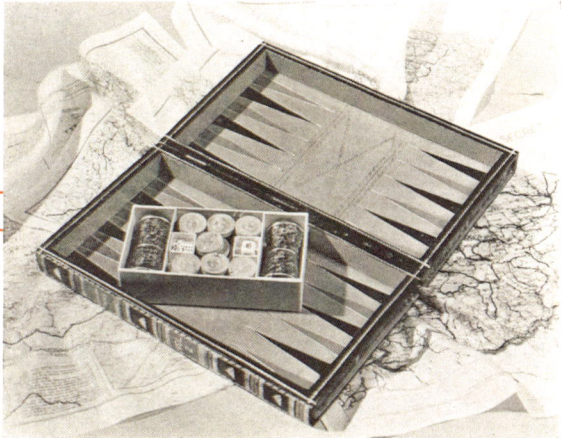

LARGE CHESS SET.

37

POST CAPTURE

GAMES CARRIERS AND THEIR CONTENTS.
(Maps and various escape aids).

TABLE TENNIS SET.

DRAUGHTS BOARD.

DOMINOES SET.

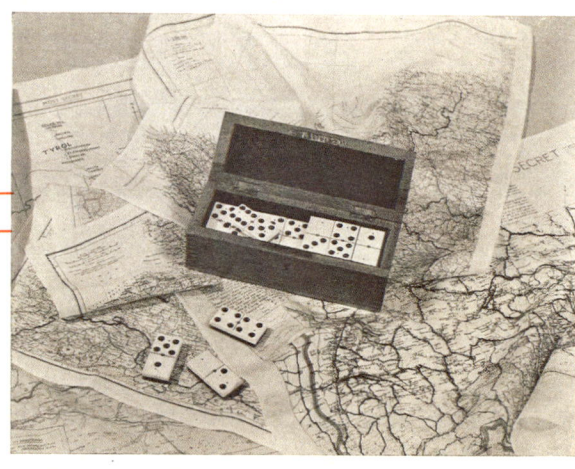

POST CAPTURE

GAMES CARRIERS.

DARTBOARD.

Each game was made by hand by the finest craftsmen, containing various escape aids.

"Doves" were used as well.

POST CAPTURE

TOILET SET CARRIERS AND THEIR CONTENTS.
(Maps and various escape aids).

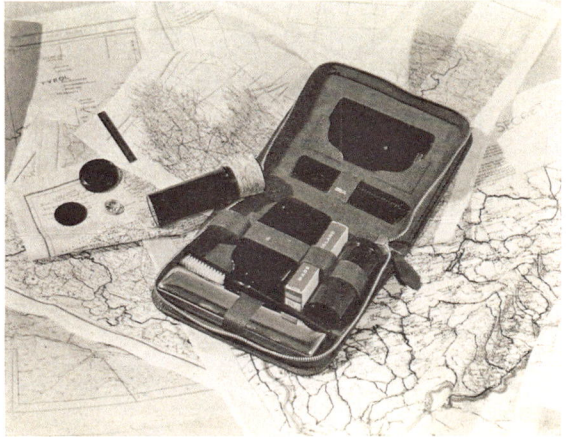

POST CAPTURE

MISCELLANEOUS CARRIERS.

STANDARD PACK OF PLAYING CARDS.

Each pack is one Map. 48 Cards covered a Map. The 4 Aces are a small Map of Europe. The Joker is the Key. The outside Card contains the instructions.

CIGAR CARRIER.

Contains either tissue or silk map and compass.

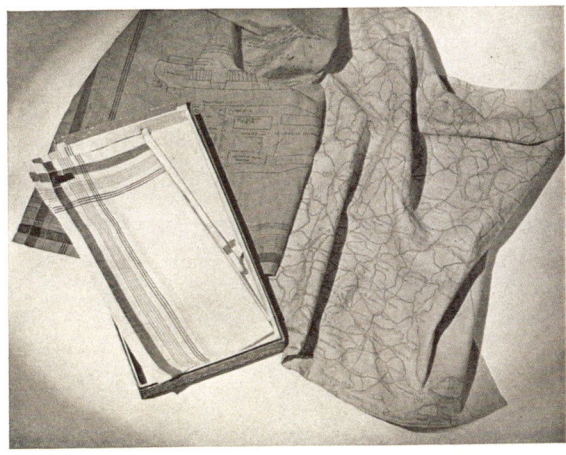

STANDARD COTTON HANDKERCHIEFS.

(Result obtained when washed with chemical on page 65.)

NEW AND SECOND HAND BOOK CARRIER.

POST CAPTURE

MISCELLANEOUS CARRIERS

TOOTH — GOLD FITTING made to measure

Small medium luminous compass fits in jaws on left and thin gold tube holding message or map slides on to the two prongs at bottom. These are concealed through being in between the cheek and gum.

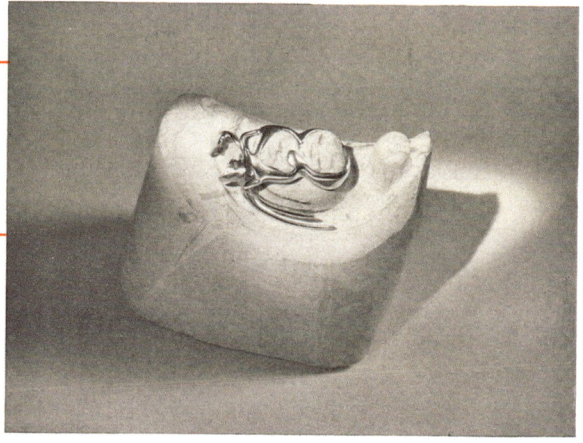

BRIDGE MARKER PENCILS AND THEIR CONTENTS.

STANDARD SANDALS

which were asked for under the name of "Picer" model.

(*Pice being Indian currency.*)

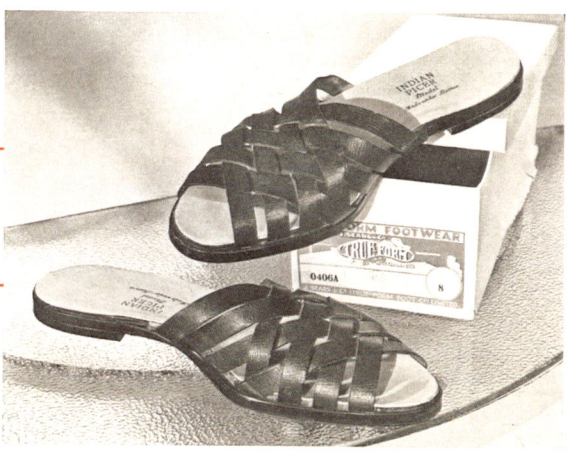

GRAMOPHONE RECORD CARRIER.

This is a standard record and contents were secreted in *both* sides. The record was perfect in every way and could be played.

ESCAPE AIDS

SPECIAL WIRELESS RECEIVERS

Cigar Box Type.   Range 400 miles.

6" x 6" x 1⅞".   Range 700 miles.

WIRELESS TRANSMITTERS

Note Telescopic 2' 6" Mast.

100 Players Cigarette Tin Type.
Range 100 miles.

POST CAPTURE

SPECIAL MESS DRESS.

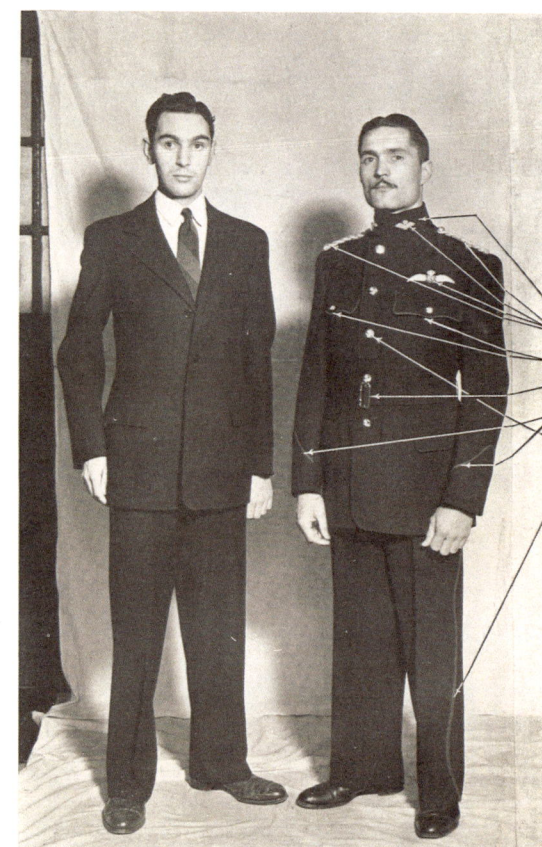

In one minute a perfect fitting walking out suit can be made — which is also waterproofed.

Take out Buckram
Take off Badges
Tear off Pockets & Flaps
Take off Belt
Tear off Sleeve Piping
Buttons replaced by those from inside Trouser Tops
Tear off Stripes

Escape Aids - A German Perspective

In 1960, Dr. Reinhold Eggers assembled a remarkable photo album documenting the escape attempts at Colditz Castle, the German prisoner-of-war (POW) camp officially known as Oflag IV-C. From November 1940 until April 1945, Eggers acted as the security officer for the castle, and became chief of security there in 1944. Following the war Dr. Eggers was imprisoned for ten years by the Russians. He was released in 1955.

Some of the album pages are displayed in the exhibition. As shown in the album pages, the ingenuity of the Allied E&E agencies in secreting escape aids was matched by that of the Germans, who discovered many of the escape aids that were sent to prisoners of war at Colditz Castle, especially after they installed an x-ray machine to check parcels sent to prisoners. The British countered this with some success by using double-walled tins of milk and other foodstuffs to hide escape aids.

The album pages show not only escape aids, but methods of escape, prisoners caught in escape costumesposing with to the person they were impersonating, and more. The album speaks for itself, although only some of the pages are shown. Album pages are shown here with the blessing of the Colditz Castle Museum.

Left: Album Title Page

Lt. Airey Neave(now MP,conservative)as a "German"Gefreiter".Mr. N. was the first English officer who made a home run.(stage attempt,together with Lt. Luteyn)Mr. N. was commandant of the Nürnberg prison.Göring,Keitel etc were his PWs.

Stage escape. Blind corridor Neave&Luteyn escaped here.

The stage escape.The hole is shut, precise won:

Dutch officer with one of the 2 busts,called "Max and Moritz".This bust was discovered in the park.(heap of leaves attempt.)

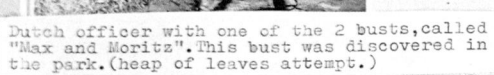

The living mail sack.

Dutch Lt. Linck leaves his hiding in the mail s

Caricature on Allan's straw sack escape by Cpt.Loizenko,by-camp.

The 6 disguised PWs have passed the sentries & leave the door.

WC-escape The 10 escapers in their kits. Standing, left: Lt. Allan, the straw sack escaper. The biggest: Lt. Hyde-Thompson, in the Franz-Joseph-escape one of the "German" soldiers. The others Elliot, Cheetham, Flinn, Middleton, Gaston (all English) Verkest and Arcq (Belgian). Karpf (Polish.)

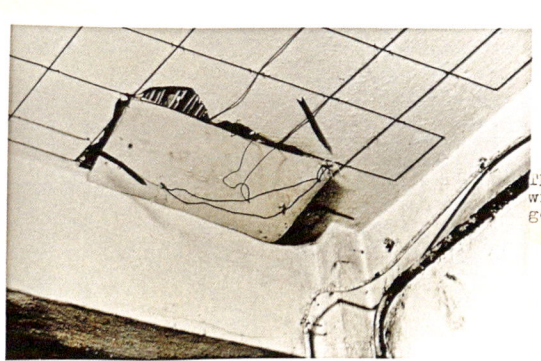
The alarming wire net bridged by a clever electrician.

WC-scene, the hole from the English quarters to a WC in the German quarters.

Lt. Boulay as a German woman, caught in German yard.

Dutch Lt. Dufour, and Lt. van Rood impersonate German officers.

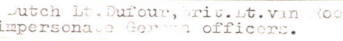

2 holl. kgf. Offiziere als deutsche Offiz. verkleidet.
Lt. Steenhove & van Lynden (Dutch) Impersonate German offic.

Belg. Lts. Verleye and Leroy are brought back to the castle when caught in the park.

Cpt. van den Heuvel, carried by Story-Pugh & Kruimininck.

The camp electrician Willy Pöhnert, called "Willy" and his double Lt. Perrodeau (left).

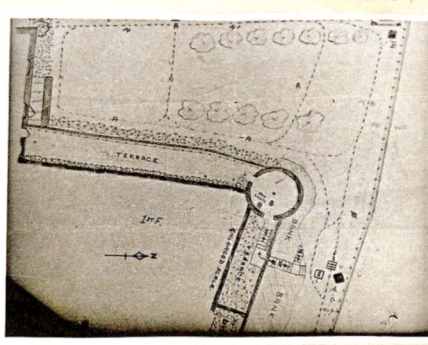

English drawing to Thom's terrace attempt.

Map of Africa. The French Radio behind it becomes visible.

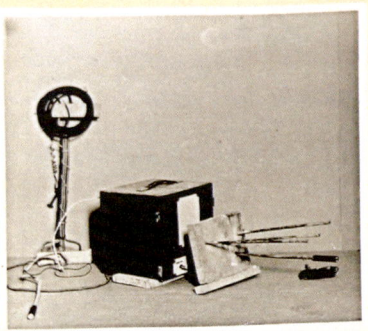

The French wireless set which was placed behind a wall with a map of Africa, smuggled into the camp by Lt. Guigues.

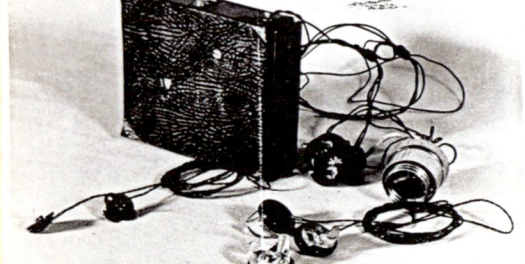

English miniature radio set, 3 valves, sent as a "dynamit parcel" from England and purloined secretly from the post office.

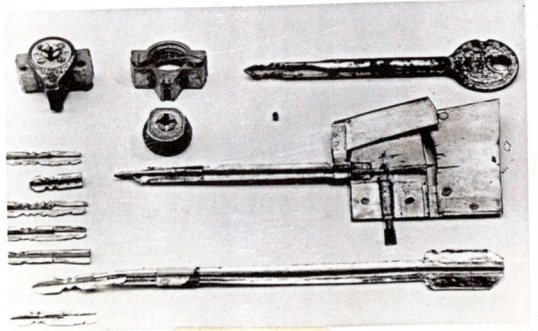

Zeiss Ikon safety key, imitation in the making.

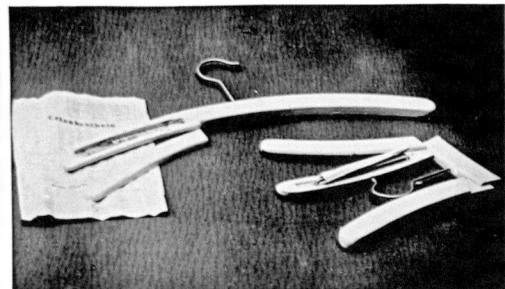

Colditz. The last cry of port habits, pattern of Mr. Clayton Hutton, Brit. War Ministry.

Colditz. No game set without Mr. Hutton's escape material.

Official leave document, sent from England. Colditz.

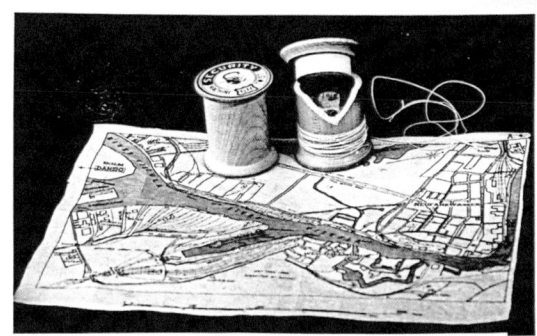

Useful threadrolls, invented by Mr. Cl. Hutton. German leave document, sent from England by H.

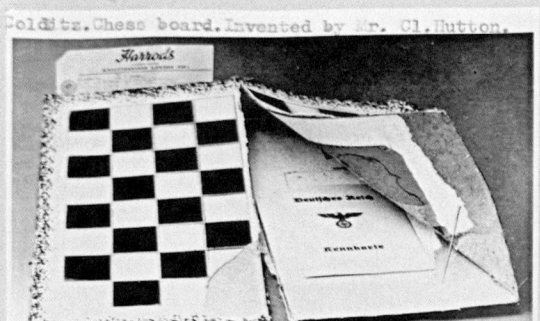

Colditz. Chess board. Invented by Mr. Cl. Hutton.

Wing commander Bader's orderly brought this chess set with him from a former PWs' camp.

A valuable nécessaire from Mr. Clayton Hutton.

A valuable calendar, invented by Mr. Cl. Hutton.

69

Grammophone record, pattern Clayton Hutton Brit.War Min.

Colditz. A nut shell with a strange kernel. Production of Mr. Cl. Hutton

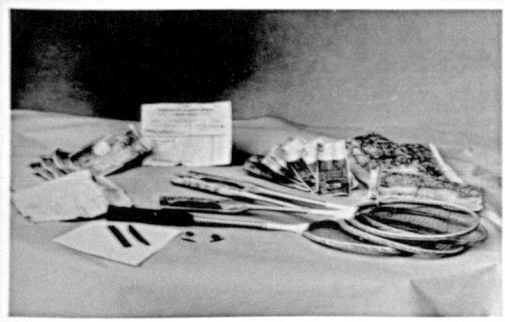

Colditz. Valuable rackets. Production of Mr.Cl.H.

Case with escape maps, made and sent by C. Hutton

Game set as hiding place for escape material, sent from the Engl. War Ministry, made by Major Clayton Hutton.

Valuable book covers, discoverd March 4th 1942. A welfare assoc. in Lisbon had sent them.

Clayton Hutton playing cards, sent via Harrods.

Colditz. Books from a welfare association in Lisbon. Valuable content in the covers.

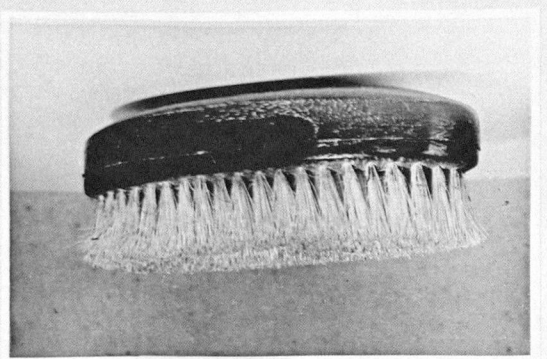
A nice harmless looking brush, pattern Cl.H.

Colditz. The brush opened. It denounces Mr. Hutter's hands. British War Ministry.

Colditz. The brush enveils its secrets.

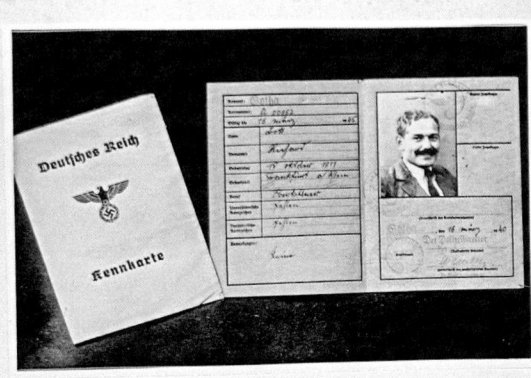
Perfect imitation of an identity document. Colditz.

Identity card, home made by the PWs.

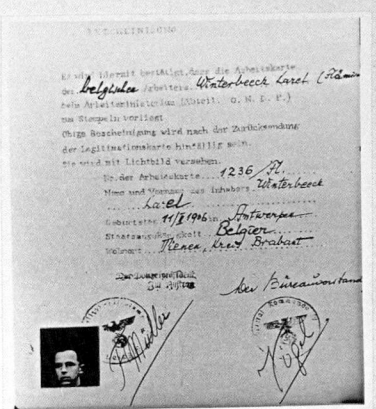
Colditz. Identity card. Made by the PWs.

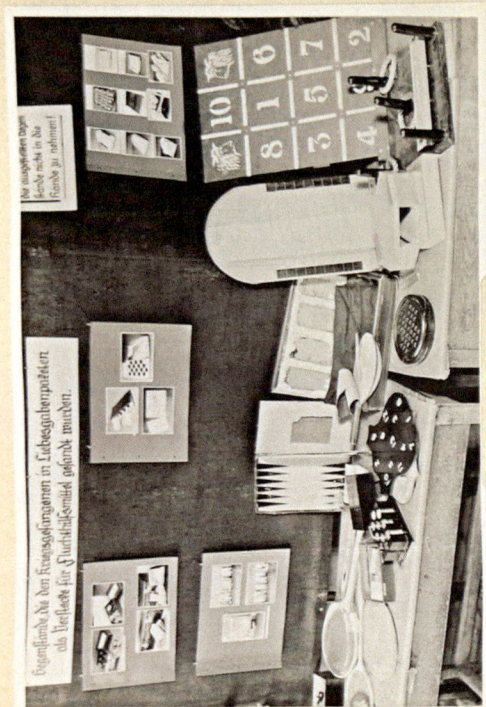
Museum Colditz Game sets as hiding places.

Men at draughts, hiding place, pow pills that cause the symptoms of Jaundice etc. Made in England by Major Clayton Hutton.

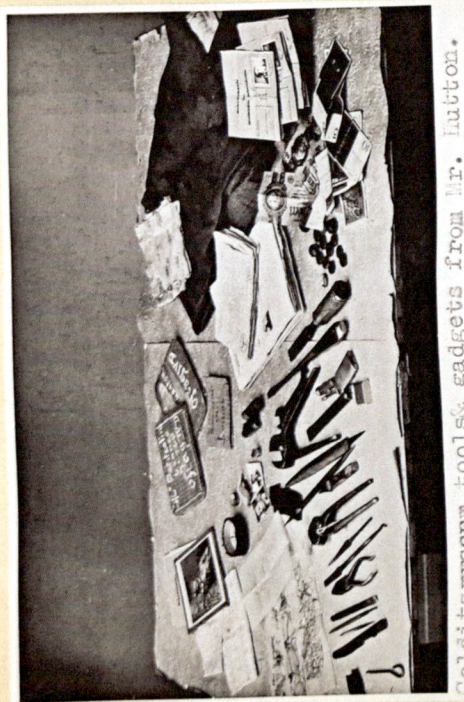
Colditzmuseum, tools & gadgets from Mr. Hutton.

View into the museum, showing the other bust and home made uniforms.

Cloth Escape Maps

There is no clear delineation between what are called *Evasion Maps* for pre-capture use and *Escape Maps* for use by prisoners of war (POWs). Many maps served both purposes. Shown here are a unique class of maps giving details of specific border crossing points and "escape routes" that could be used to find one's way to places to obtain help from local partisans and others. Maps like these were sent into POW camps secreted in everyday-looking objects, which is why they are referred to in this exhibition as "Escape Maps." It is unlikely that most of these maps would have been issued to air crews, because if discovered on an evader, the enemy would have tightened security along the routes and at border crossings shown. For the same reason, these maps would not have been taken out of camp by escaping prisoners. Instead, POWs made their own hand-drawn copies of maps to take with them on escapes. Though no longer classified, many are marked "Secret" and "Most Secret" for obvious reasons.

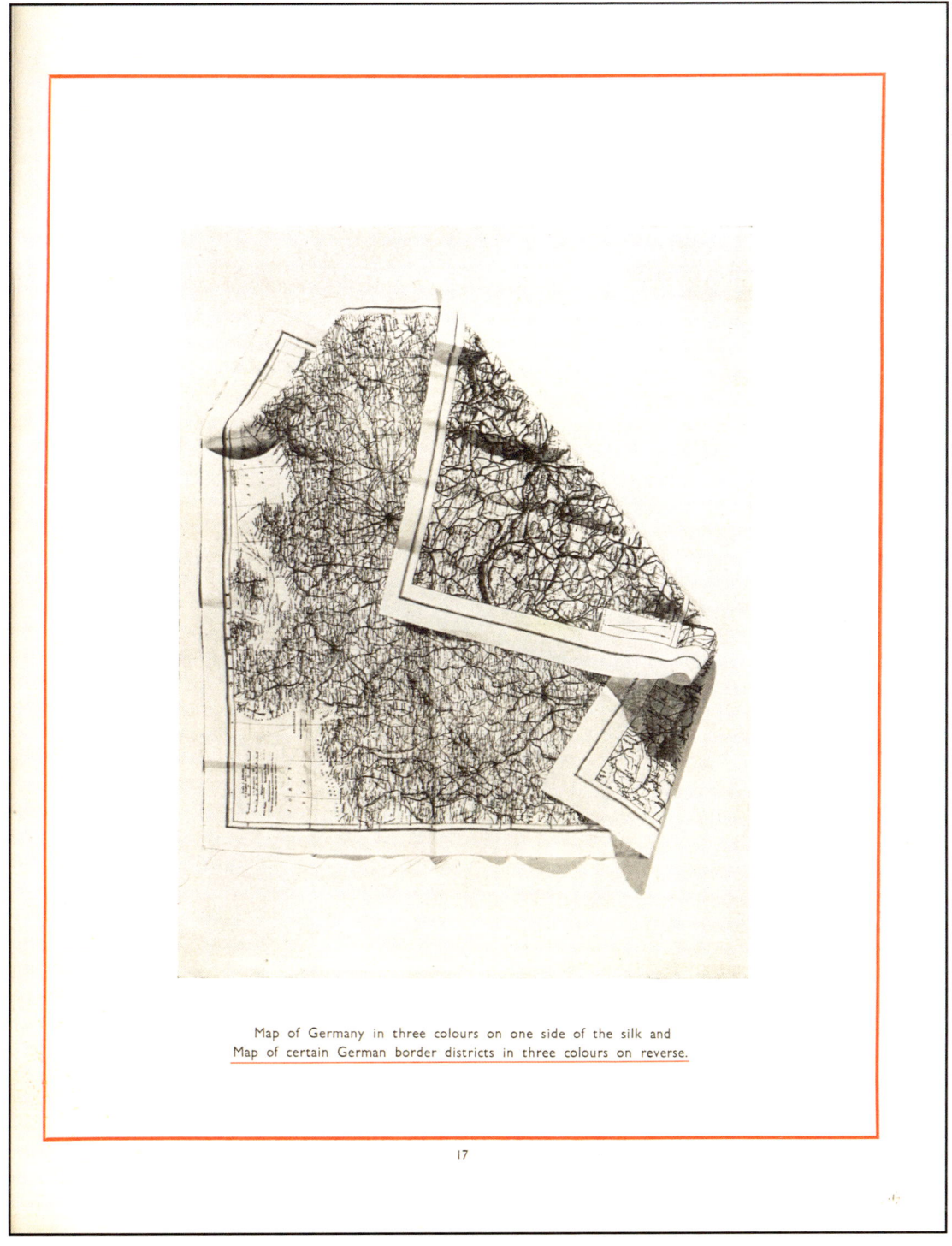

A page from *Per Aruda Libertas* showing a silk map with German border area details on the reverse of a map of Germany.

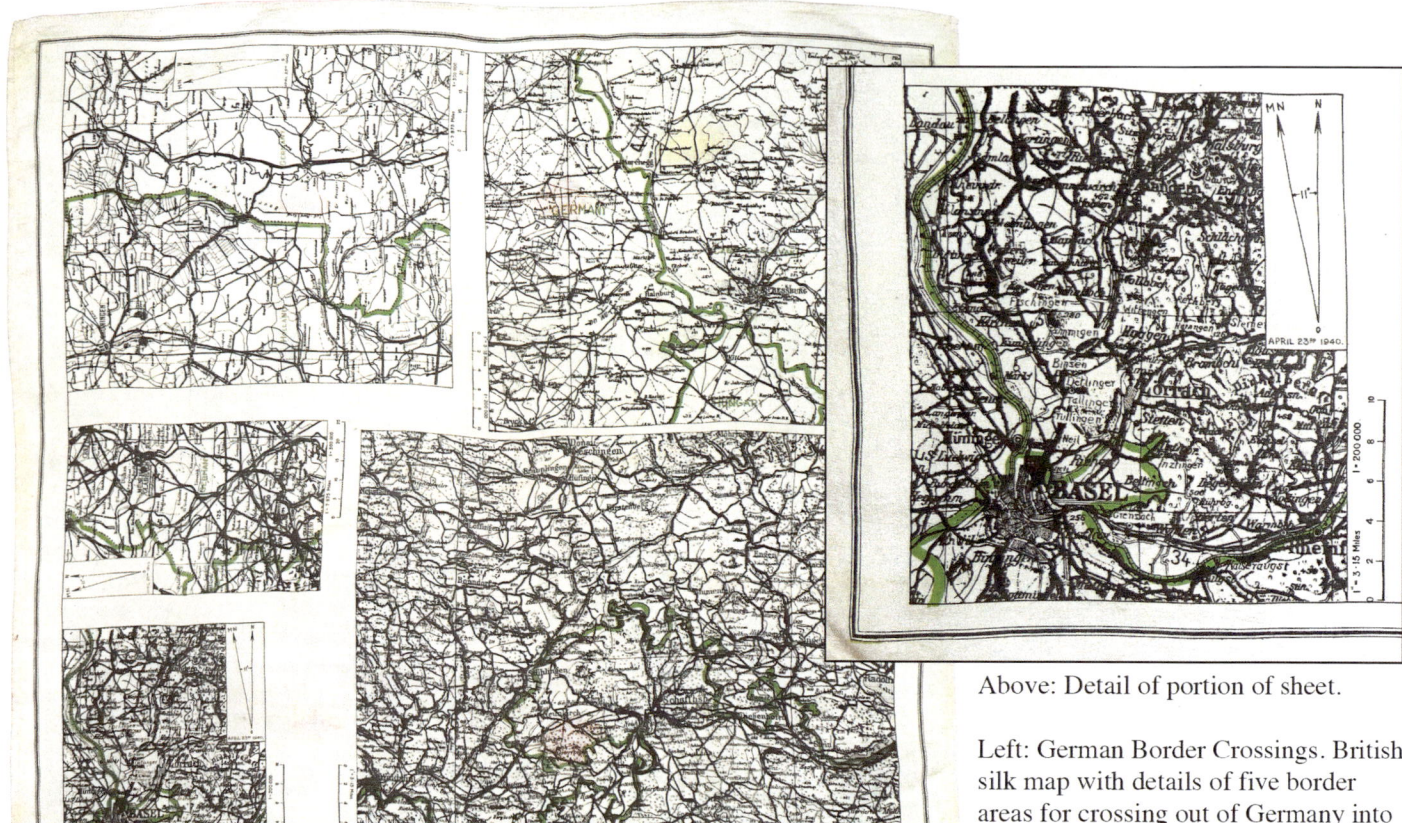

Above: Detail of portion of sheet.

Left: German Border Crossings. British silk map with details of five border areas for crossing out of Germany into Switzerland, Holland, and Czechslovakia, dated April 23. 1940.

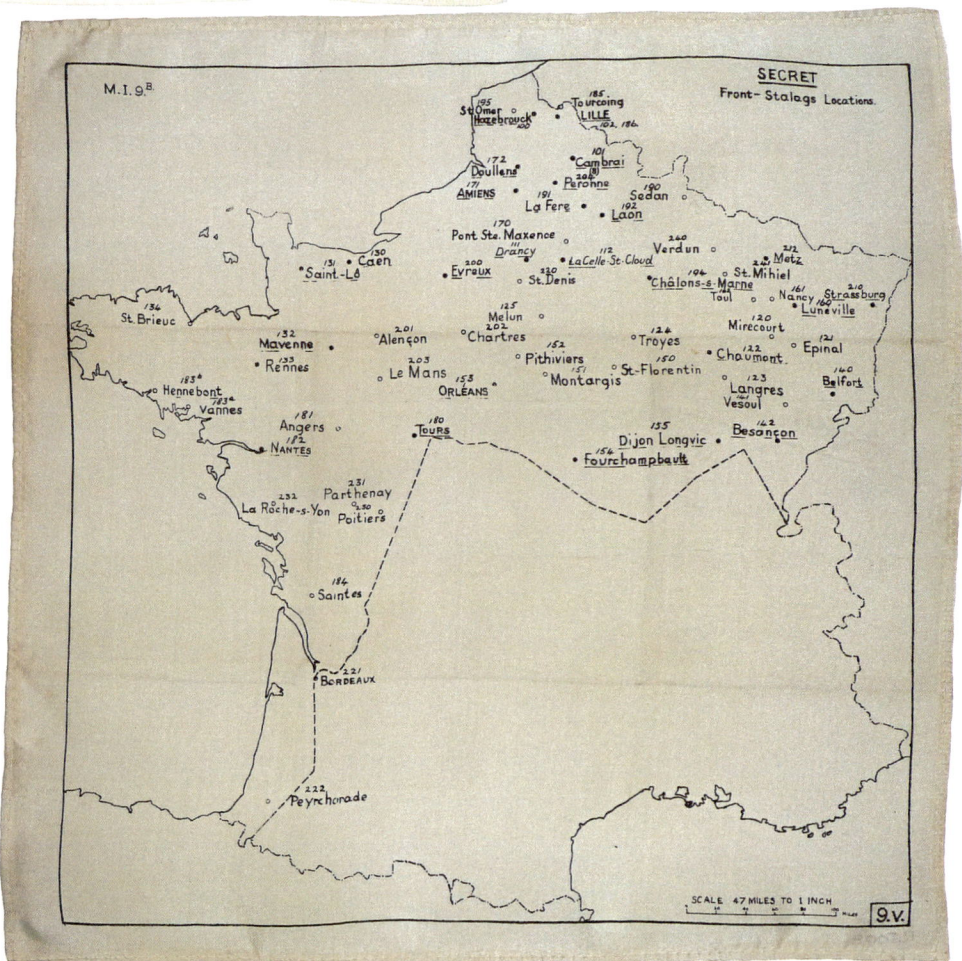

Right: Sheet 9V. Silk map showing POW camps in the German military occupied zone of France. The specific purpose of this map is unknown. It is the only map known to be marked with the name MI9.

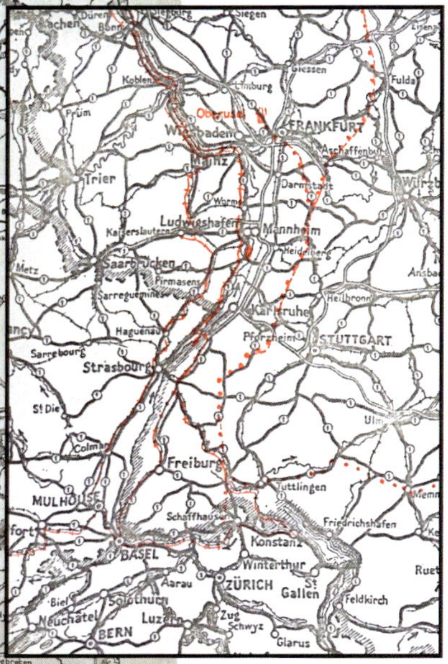

Above: Sheet 9UR. Silk map of Germany and portions of France, Poland, and Switzerland, with specific features including railroads, barge routes, and escape routes shown in red. The end of one escape route is Salzburg, Austria, and from there an escaper could use map Sheet X to find their way to Yugoslavia.
Above Right: Detail of a portion of 9UR.

Right: Norway Border Crossings Sheet: Artificial silk map of Norway with the best points for crossing into the eastern zone occupied by German troops underlined. From the eastern zone escapers could make their way to neutral Sweden.
Below: Detail of Norway Border Crossings Sheet.

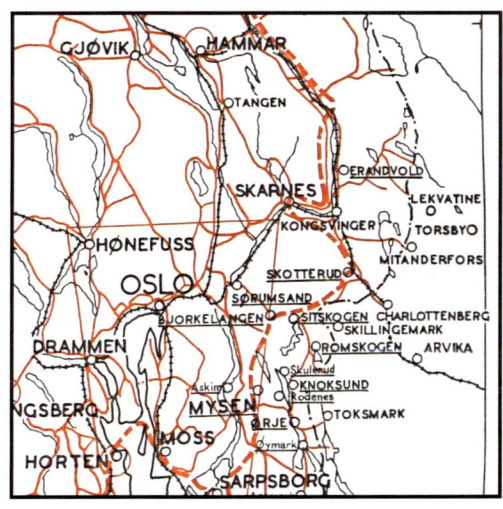

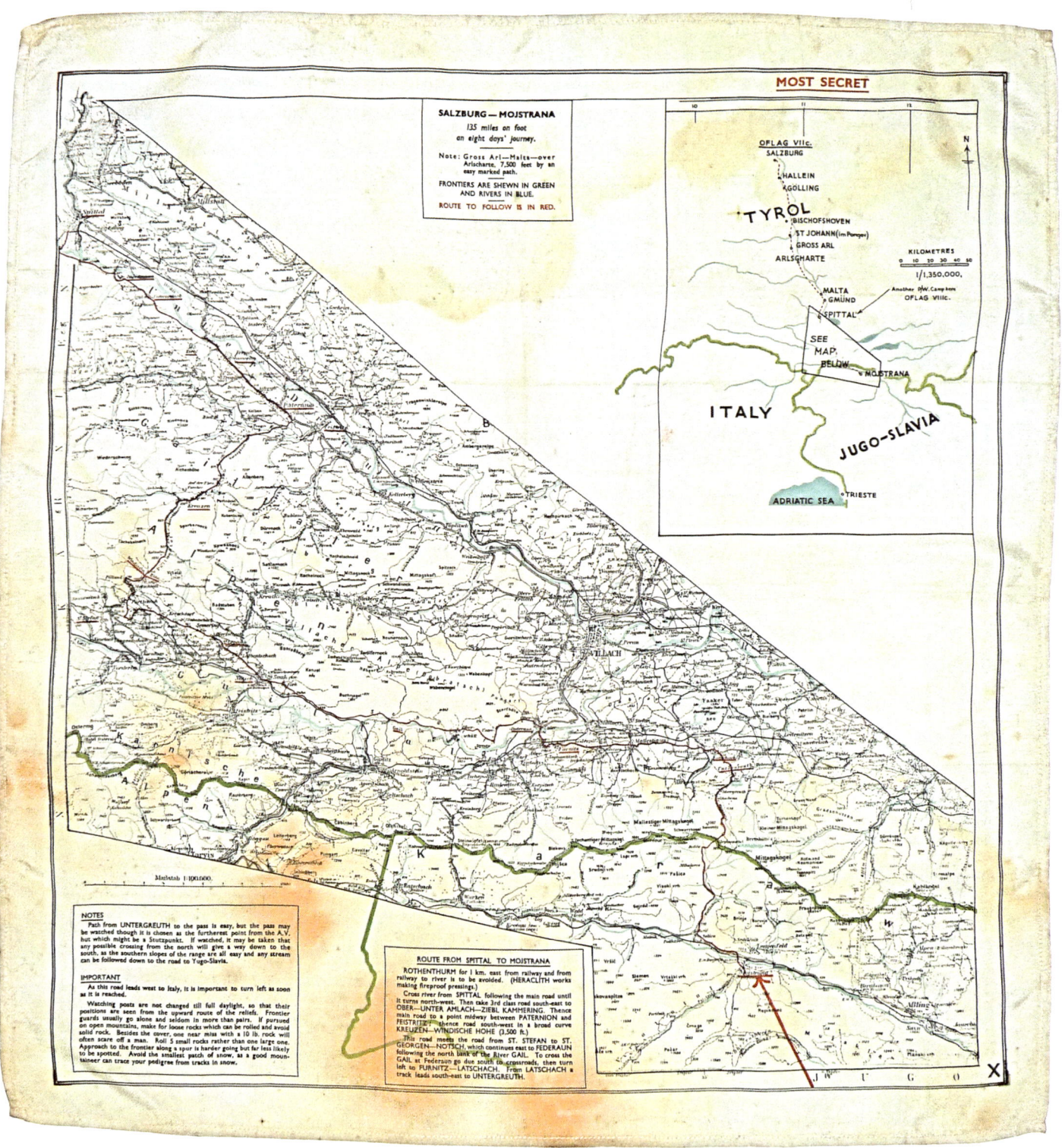

Sheet X: British silk map detailing the escape route from Salzburg, Austria, to Mojstrana, Yugoslavia. The actual route is shown on the map in red, along with detailed notes and instructions for following the route.

Sheet Y: British silk map detailing the escape route through southern Germany to Canton Schaffhausen in Switzerland. The actual route is shown on the map in red (>>>), along with detailed instructions for using the route.

Sheet Y2: Artificial silk map, basically a strip map in two sections detailing the border area between southern Germany and Canton Schaffhausen. This gives more detail than Sheet Y. On the reverse of this sheet is Sheet 9Y3, which is identical to Sheet Y3.

Sheet Y3: This silk map is the most detailed map of the actual crossing into Canton Schaffhausen, complete with topography, including contours. The route is shown in red (>>>). The map is oriented correctly with north at the top of the page.

Tissue Paper Escape Maps

The advantage to printing maps on tissue paper was that they could be folded small and were thus easily secreted in parts of the uniform and in common objects in order to be available to personnel after they had been captured and arrived in camp. Two types of tissue paper were used: mulberry paper had the advantage of not deteriorating even when submerged in water, and it did not make noise when crumpled up; rice paper dissolved easily in water so that in a pinch it could be eaten if that was the only option available to keep it from being discovered by the enemy. All of the maps shown here are printed on rice paper.

Britain pioneered the use of tissue paper maps, but at least 35 different maps were printed in the US on rice paper under contract with MIS-X, some of them at the request of Britain.

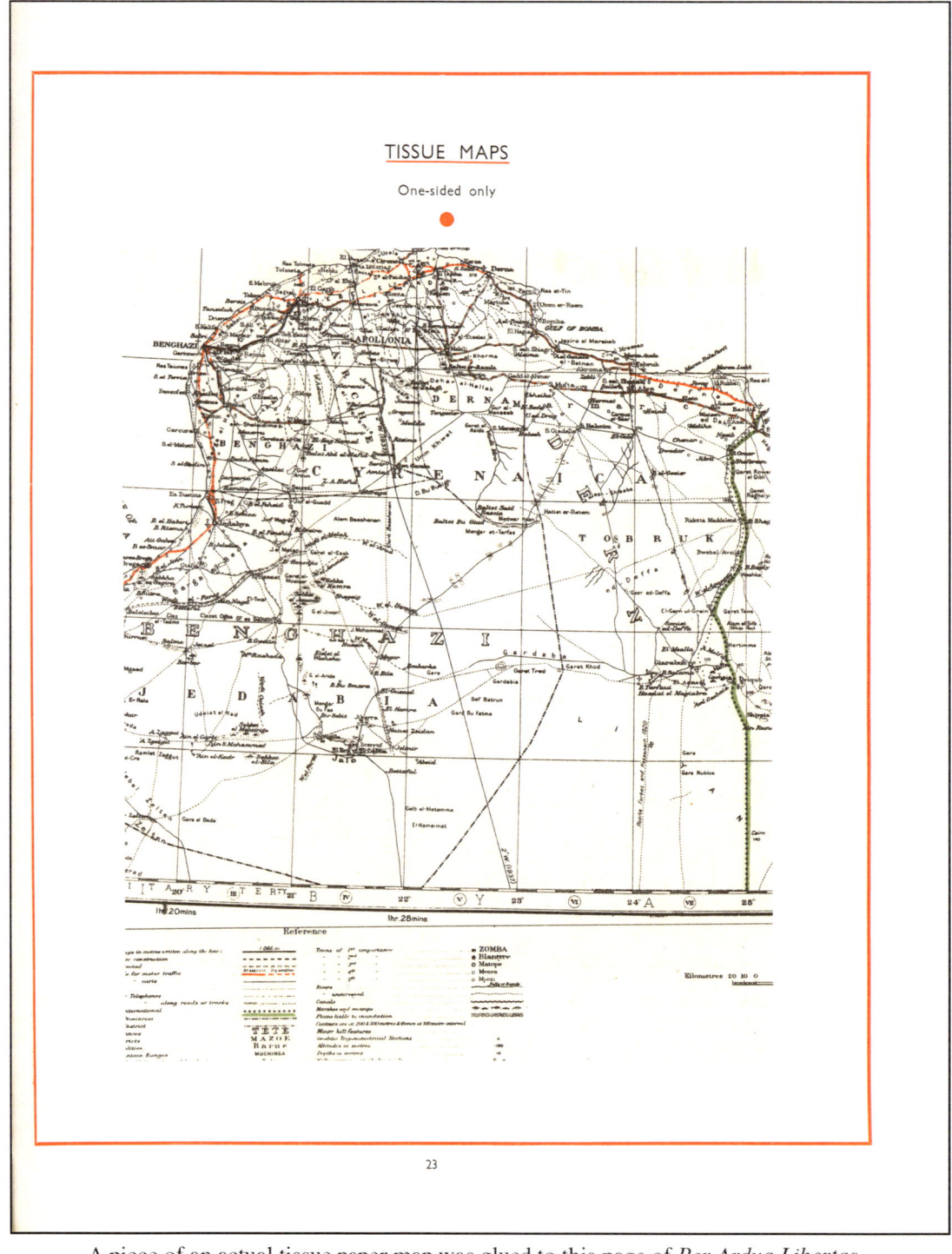

A piece of an actual tissue paper map was glued to this page of *Per Ardua Libertas*.

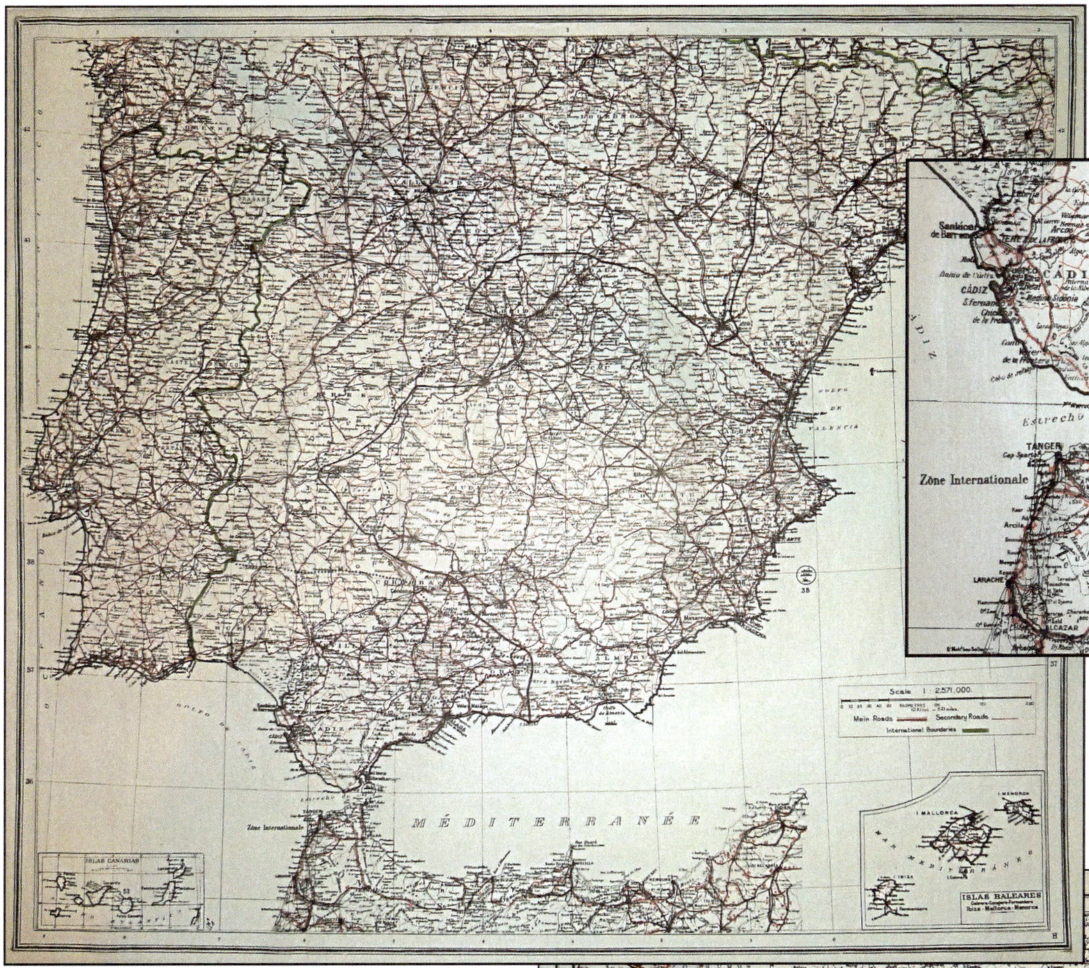

Detail of Sheet H

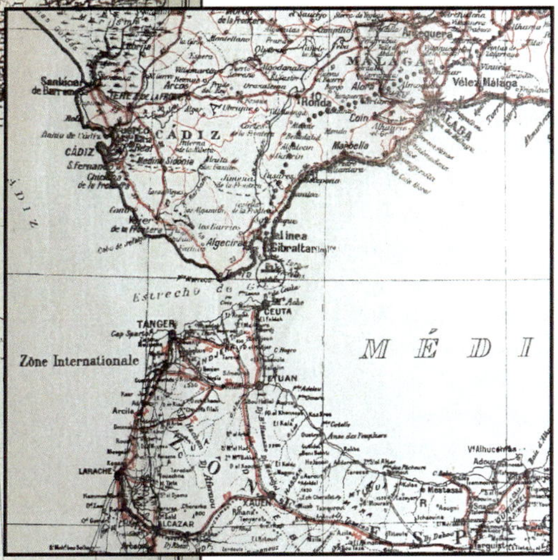

Above: British map sheet H, Spain and Portugal, with Tangier and a portion of Spanish Morocco.

Right: British map sheet O, covering Abyssinia in eastern Africa, which was invaded and occupied by Italy in 1935.

Detail of Sheet O

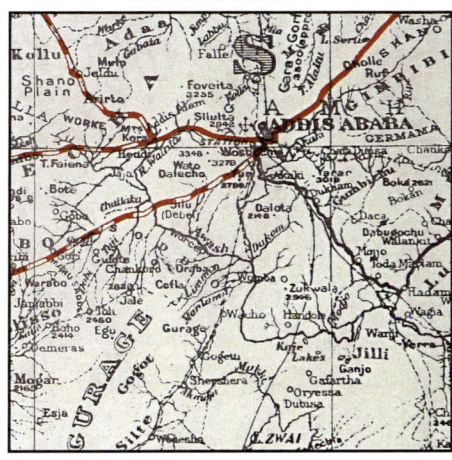

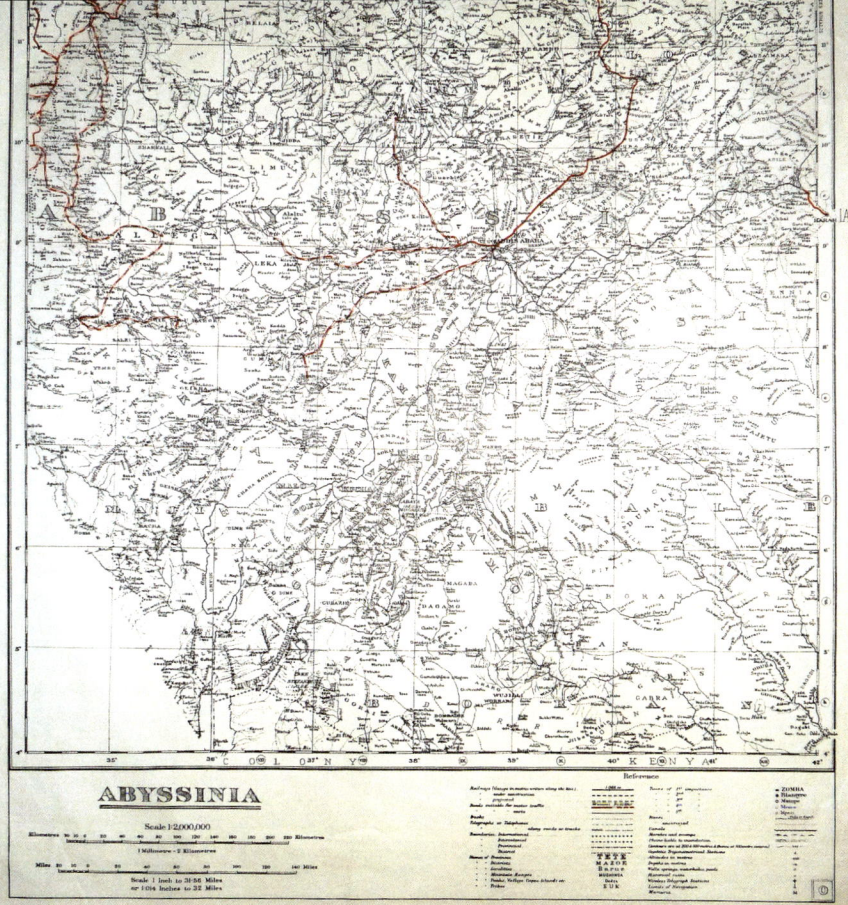

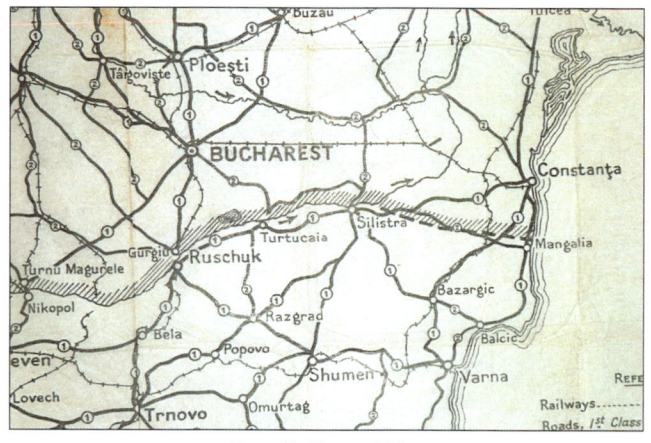

Detail Sheet 9T.

Right: British Air Ministry Sheet 9T, *Bulgaria and Roumania*. Ploesti, just north of Bucharest, was the target Operation Tidal Wave, one of the costliest air missions of the war when US Army Air Force B-24 bombers based in Libya attacked the Ploesti Astra Romana oil refinery.

Left: Tissue map sheet of Magdeburg, near Stalag XIa Altengabrow, was printed in the US and is one in a series of detailed maps of areas around prisoner-of-war camps.

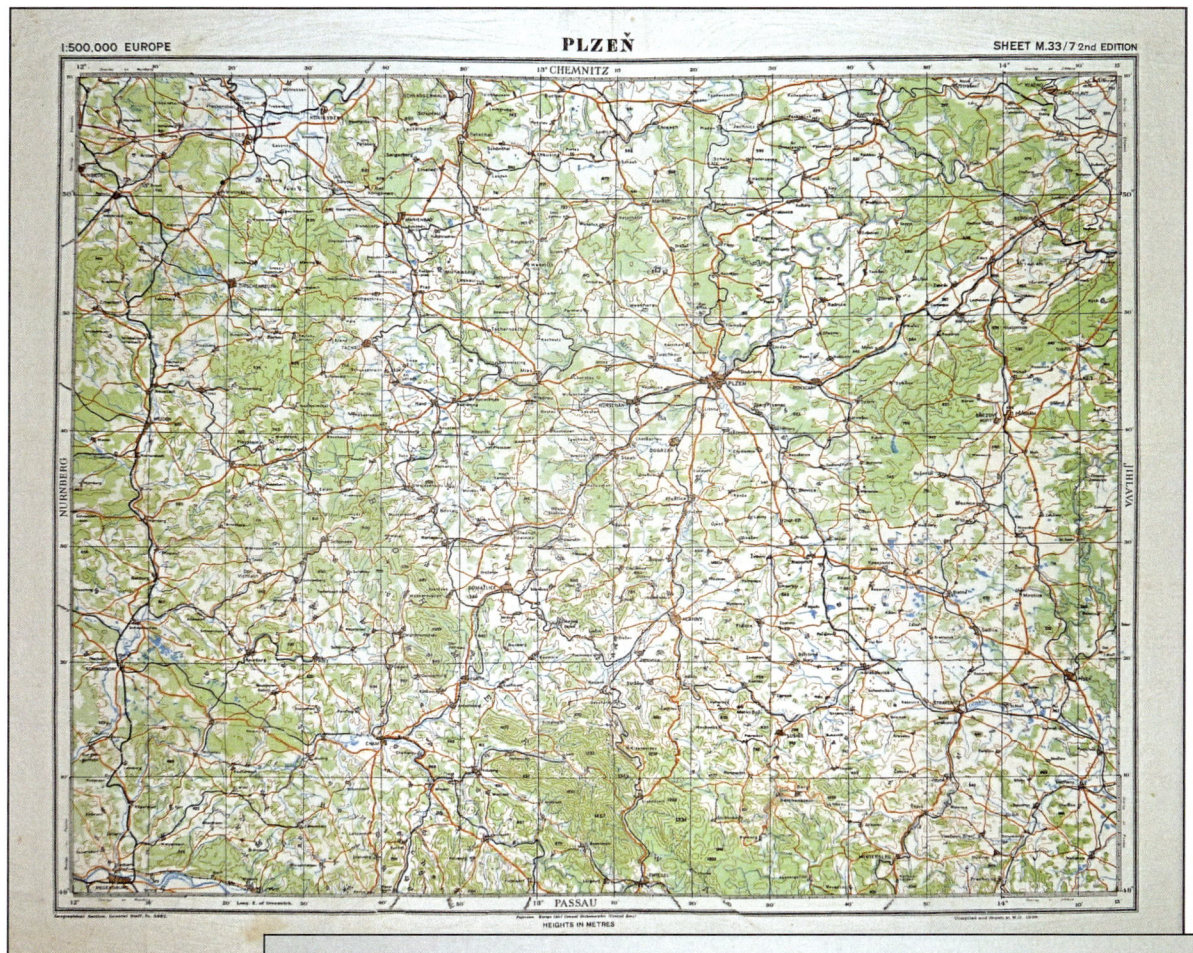

Above: This small, detailed map of Plzen, Czechoslovakia, was printed in the US.

Right: British Air Ministry Sheet 9U, Germany and part of Poland, and a good overview of the areas where many prisoner-of-war camps were located.

The *Sagan* sheet is one in a series of highly detailed maps of areas around prisoners-of-war camps, Sagan was the home of Stalag Luft III, the camp made famous by "The Great Escape" in which 76 prisoners escaped. This large sheet is one of the tissue maps printed in the US, and was obtained from the son of a MIS-X veteran.

British tissue map of Tripolitania, one of the areas in North Africa that, like Cyrenaicia, is still referred to by its ancient Roman name. This map sheet was made from a French map of the area with French and Romanized Arabic place names, overprinted with a legend in English. Sources of water are printed in blue.

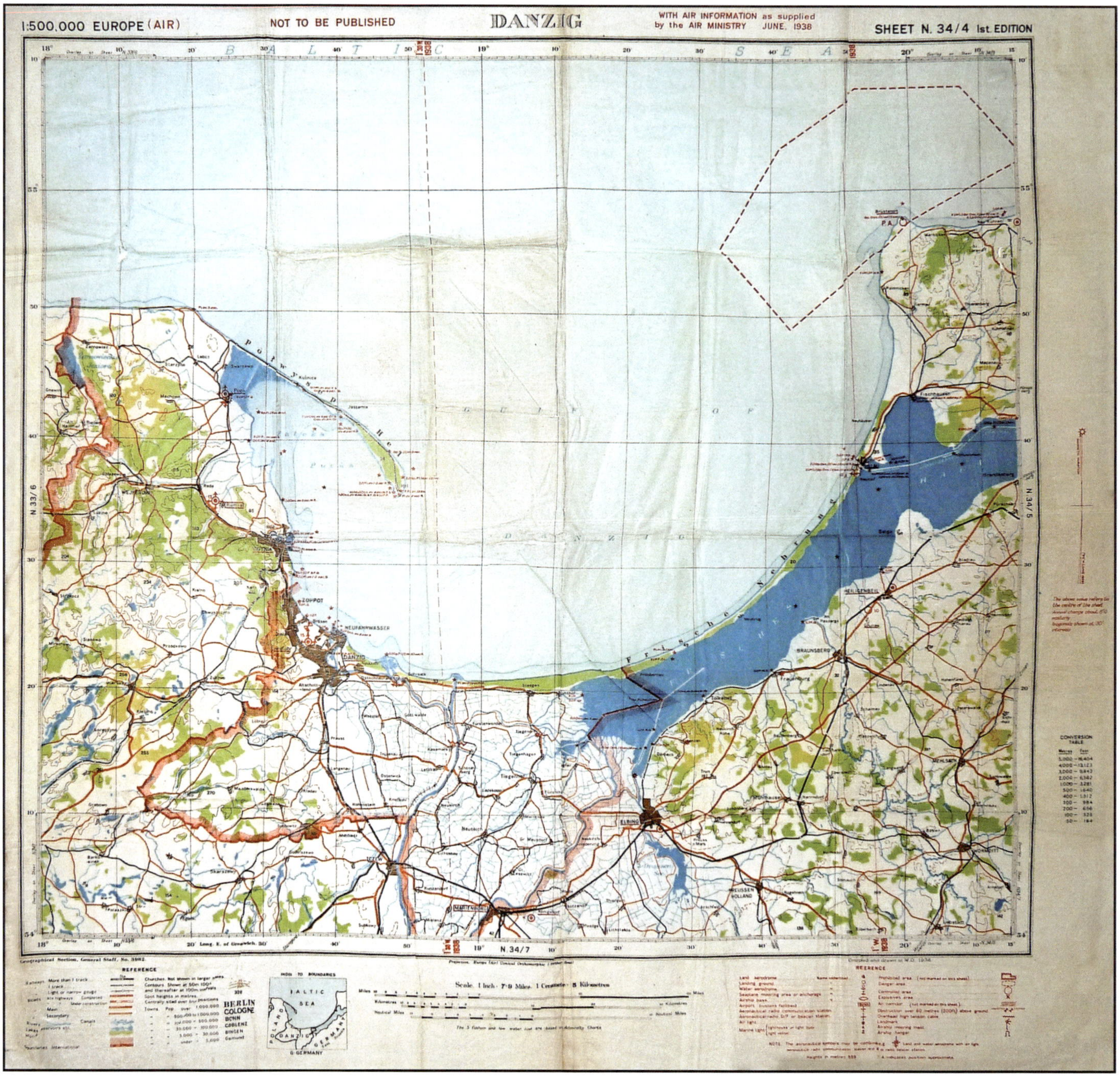

Map sheet *Danzig* is one of the "Air Miniature" series of silk maps that was also printed on tissue. The harbors in Danzig and Gdynia, two towns shown on this sheet, were destinations for escapers because ships bound for neutral Sweden could be found there. Gdynia is the subject of tissue map sheet A10, an extremely small map found elsewhere in this exhibition.

Detail of map sheet *Danzig*.

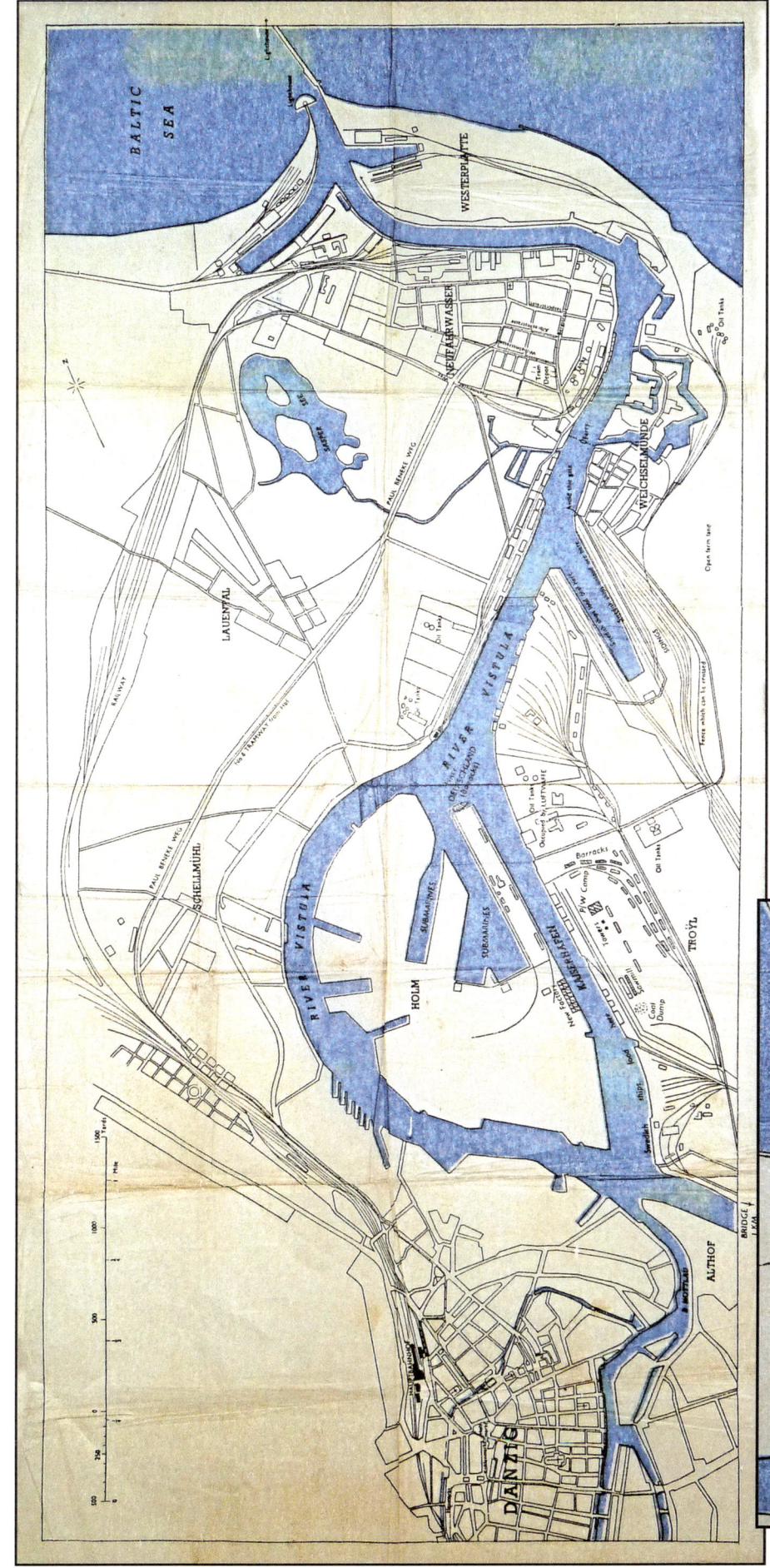

This is the British version of the tissue map of Danzig Harbor. The version printed later in the US was more detailed. The area with the words "Swedish ships load here" was the destination for escapers attempting to board a ship to neutral Sweden.

Detail of a portion of the Danzig Harbor map.

Escape Aids

Escape Aids (post-capture aids) were of little use in the brutal Prisoner of War (POW) camps in Asia. In the POW camps in Germany, however, they proved their worth. Clandestine escape aids were concealed in uniforms worn by aircrews, and in everyday objects sent into POW camps by Allied E&E agencies posing as "prisoner aid" societies.

In addition to original escape aids, this exhibit uses educational items made from original period items to illustrate how ordinary objects could be utilized to hide them.

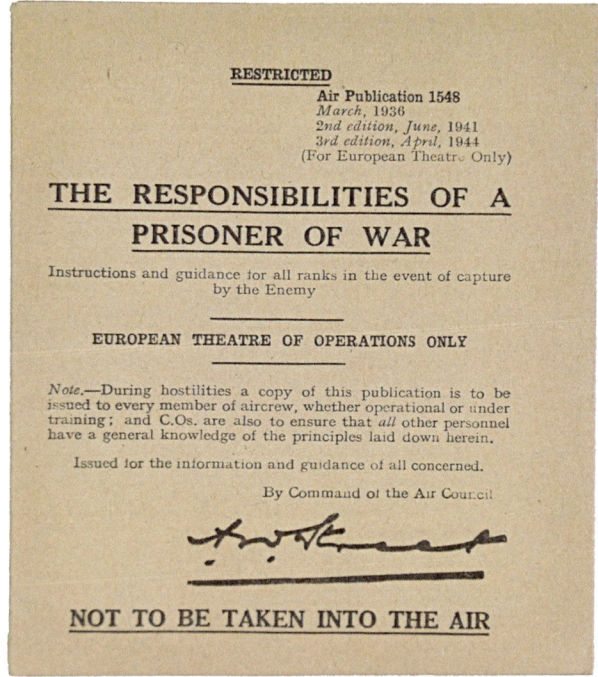

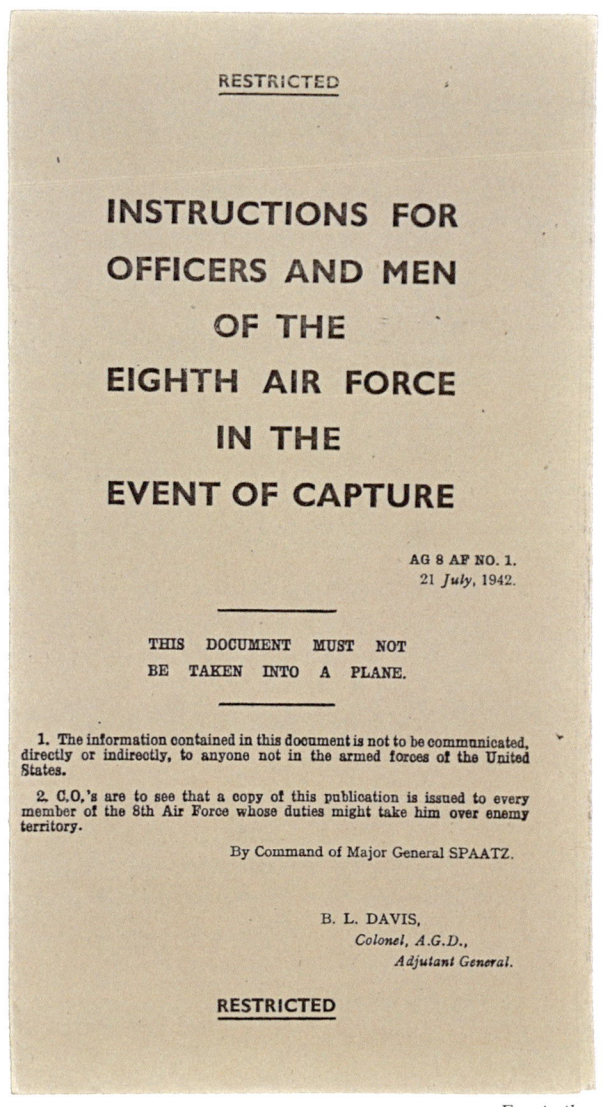

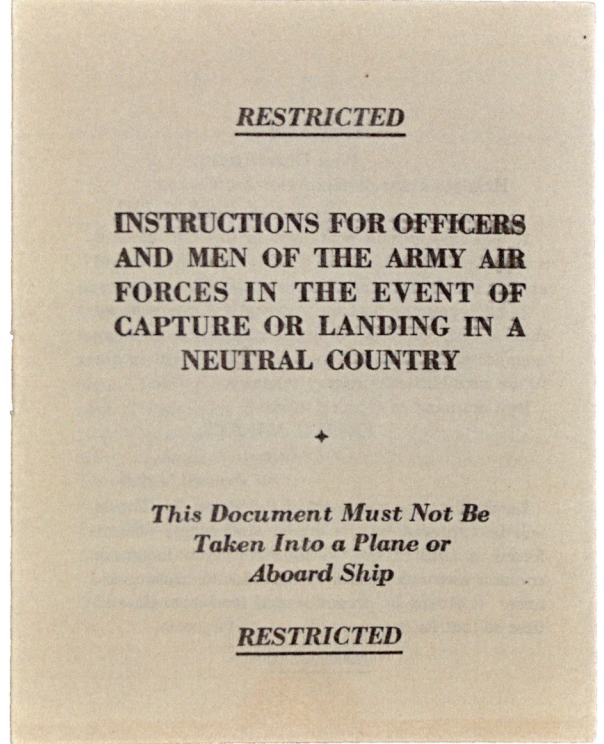

Facsimile

Allied E&E agencies provided essential training to airmen and others on what to expect and how to behave if captured. Shown here are examples of some of the booklets and folded pamphlets that were distributed to personnel. Note that they were not to be taken into combat lest the enemy discover the Allied instructions for behavior and for resisting interrogation.

209,000 MAPS

AND

214,000 AIDS ITEMS

FOR

PRE AND POST CAPTURE

WERE DISTRIBUTED
UP TO FEBRUARY 14th, 1942
TO UNITS OF THE THREE SERVICES

MAKING A TOTAL OF

423,000 AIDS

This page from *Per Ardua Libertas* gives the total number of aids distributed by MI9 during the first two years of the agency's work.

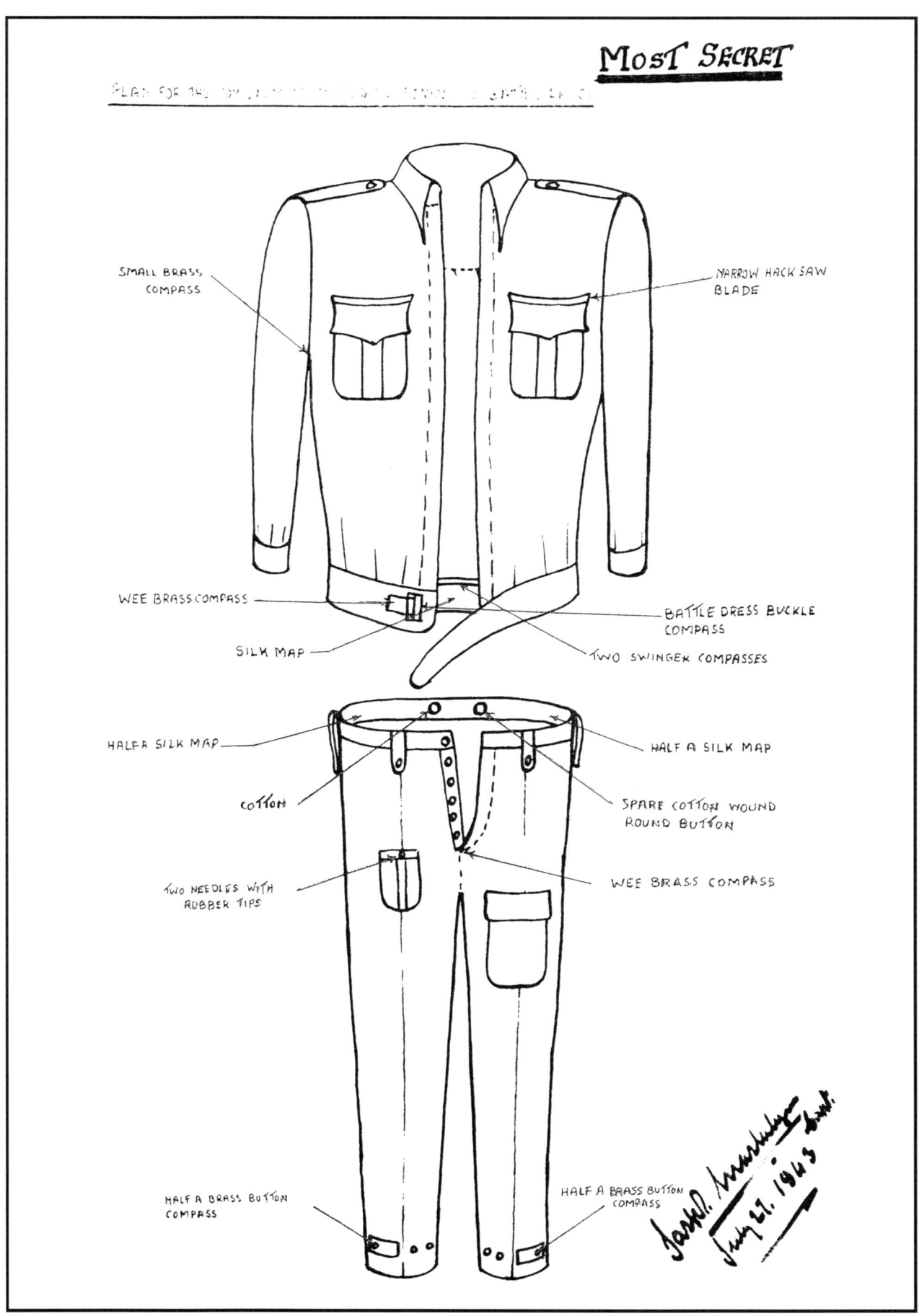

This illustration from A-Force in North Africa was provided to E&E briefers as an example of where escape aids could be hidden in battle dress. The title of the drawing is not readable.

A map and compass were essential for escape, so many forms of compasses were produced.

Five variations of British compasses that were included in evasion and survival kits, as well as in escape aids. The two at the right are known in Asia as DEC-3. (DEC, DEB, DEM, AND DES designations for escape aids were apparently used only in Asia.)

Miniature British compasses. Any or all of the three on the left may be DEC-9, described only as "medium." Two views of the compass with a screw, DEC-1 in Asia, are shown. Documents say the screw is for holding the compass. Approximate dimensions in mm, left to right, ø denotes diameter: 7.5ø x 5.9, 7.2ø x 4.8, 7.5ø x 3.7, 7.3ø x 4.8 (not including screw).

Miniature compass in original issue envelope, possibly DEC-2, officially described as "midget." Approx. 6.2ø x 4.1 mm.

Three American compasses. The two on the left were used in evasion and survival kits. The one on the right was hidden in an Army uniform button.

British brass "Fly Button" compasses. One of them magnetized so it could be balanced on the other one with a spike. The plain brass buttons are known as DEC 6 in Asia. Those painted black for the RAF, known as DEC-5, are shown balanced to make the compass. At right is a pair as issued, wrapped in tissue paper, with a rubber guard over the spike.

Three colors of British Battle Dress button compasses with magnetic material embedded in the back. Left to Right: brown, brown-green, black.

Fly Button compasses were shipped in bulk sewn to cardboard.

Battle dress button compasses were shipped in bulk attached to cardboard.

Many compasses were shipped in bulk in boxes.

By late in the war, every razor blade sold in British military exchanges was magnetized for use as a compass.

Two versions of "swinger" compasses that could be suspended on thread, designated DEC-4 in Asia. These were issued in pairs wrapped in tissue paper, as shown on the right.

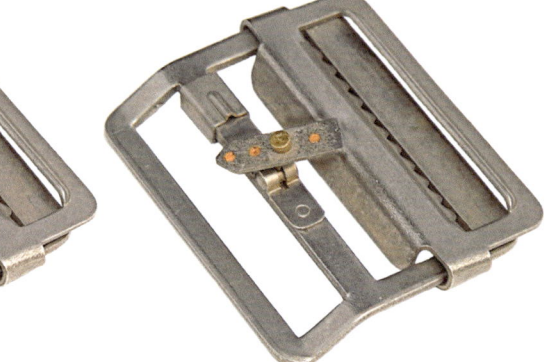

British Battle Dress buckle compass. Left: As removed from uniform. The compass parts would have been hidden by the belt. Right: Compass assembled for use.

Five British escape compasses. Left to right: A magnetized phonograph needle, two miniature compasses that could be balanced on a needle or other sharp object, a magnetized pencil clip, known as DEC-14, and a magnetized pen nib, both with "dimples" on which they could be balanced.

Above: Two British collar stud compasses. Paint was removed to reveal the compass hidden beneath

Right: Tunic buttons that unscrewed to reveal a hidden compass were produced for different branches of the British armed forces. The images at the right show the button in the process of being unscrewed, and the button with the compass removed. More of these compasses are shown on the following page.

Royal Air Force (RAF) tunic button and sidecap button compasses, side by side for size comparison.

RAF tunic button compass.

RAF sidecap button compass.

Royal Canadian Air Force tunic button compass.

Artillery tunic button compass.

Royal Marines button compass.

General service button compass. This may be a vanity piece rather than an issue item.

Branch of service unknown to our guest curator. Perhaps a vanity piece, although it has a left-hand thread.

Note: Once the enemy discovered tunic button compasses, MI9 reversed the thread from right-hand to left-hand so that when the enemy was checking a button the compass was actually being tightened.

Hinged U.S. Army (including Army Air Force) tunic button compass.

U.S. Navy button compass, likely a vanity piece as no record of such an item being issued has been found.

Royal Marines cap badge with hidden compass. As collecting E&E items has become more popular, more and more inauthentic items are being sold, this being one of the easiest to fabricate. This was acquired some time ago, yet without provenance.

Small British thrusting weapon hidden in a pencil.

Two cigarette lighters containing hidden compasses.

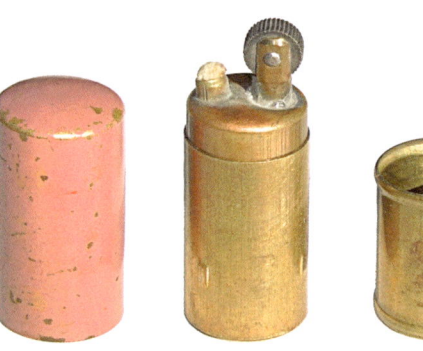

Cigarette lighter with an extra compartment concealing a compass.

British issue cigarette lighter with a secret compartment with a left-hand thread beneath the tall, thin flint container, unscrewed to reveal a compass.

Miniature British telescopes for watching prison guards.

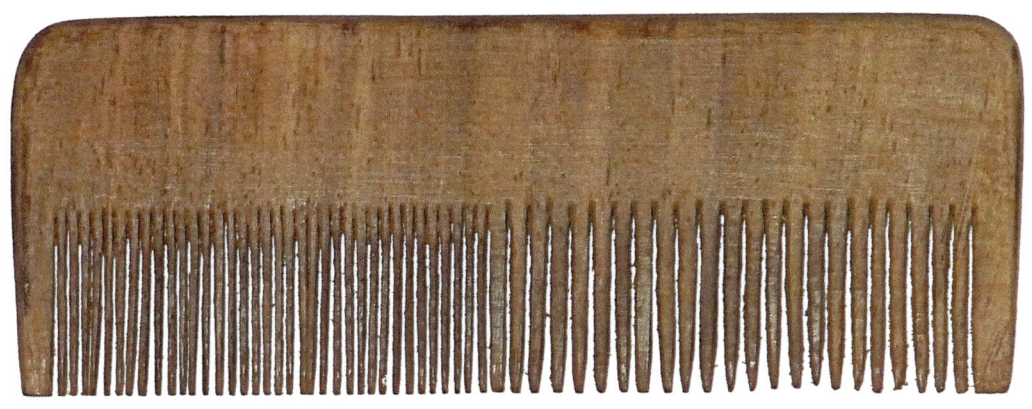
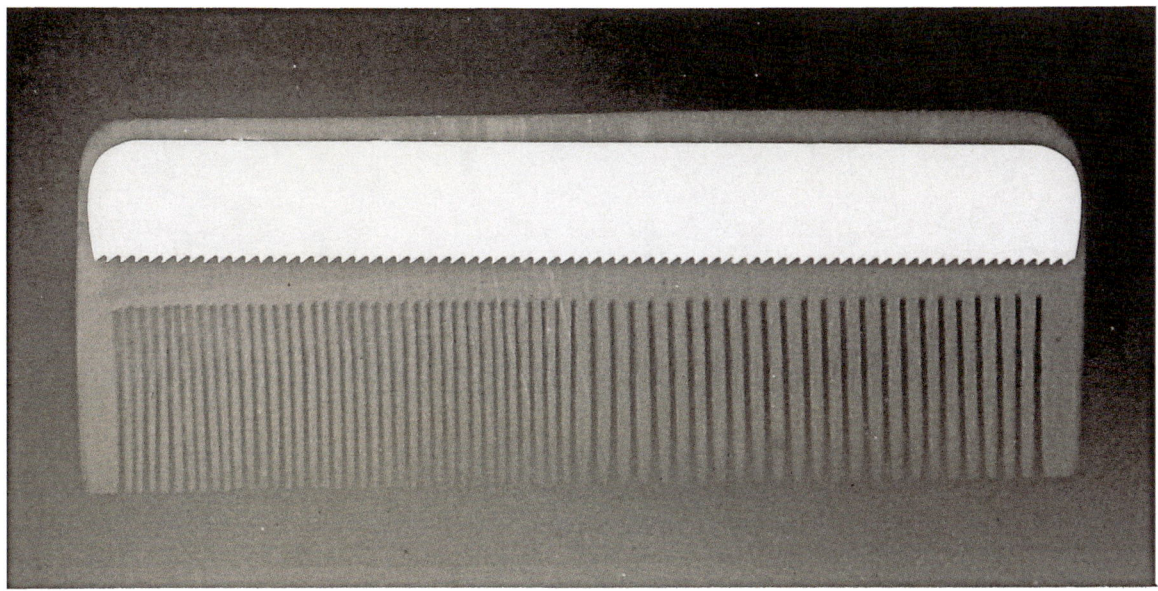

This wooden comb, known as "DES 2" in Asia, conceals a hacksaw as shown in the accompanying X-Ray. *Special thanks to Matt Wehling who provided the X-Ray of a similar comb.*

This British tobacco pouch carried by Paul Adams, whose photo and identity disk are also shown, conceals a cloth map.

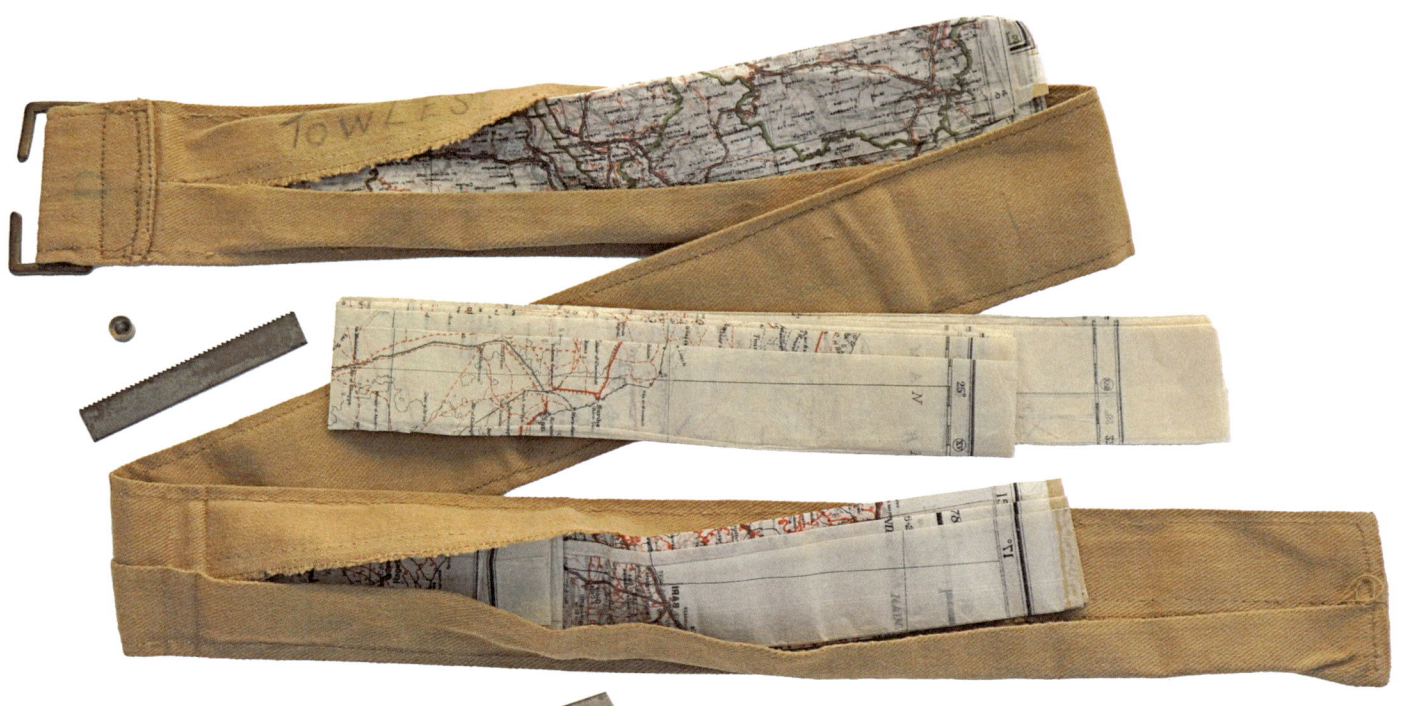

Above: This belt conceals two tissue maps of Italy, a tissue map of Cyrenaica, a hacksaw blade, and a compass.

Left: Detail of the hacksaw blade and compass from the belt shown above.

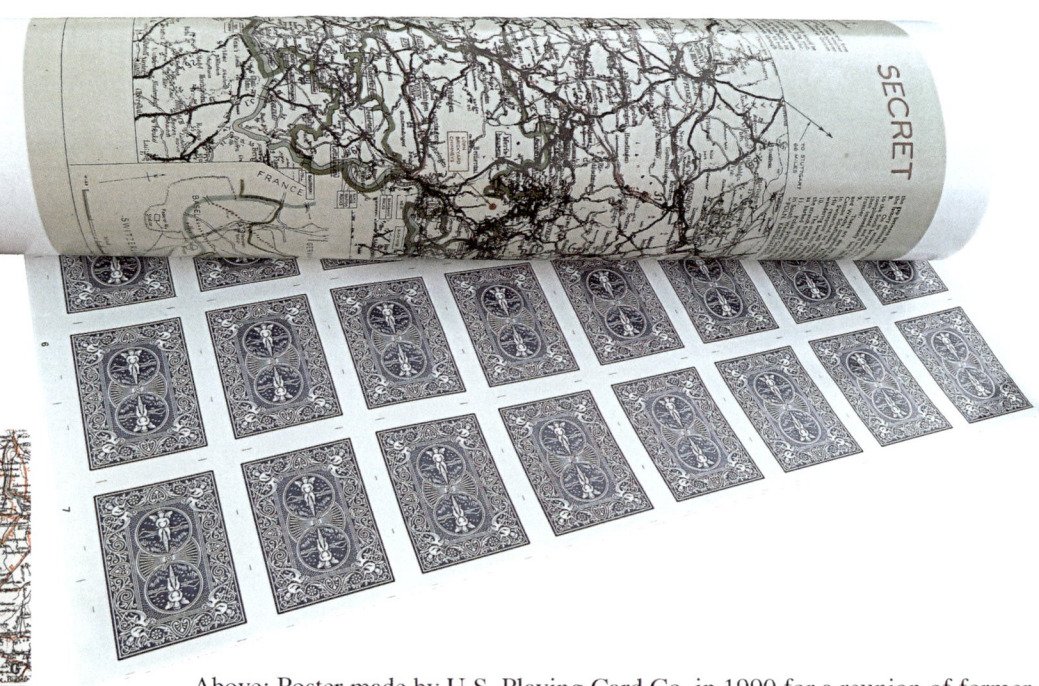

Above: Poster made by U.S. Playing Card Co. in 1990 for a reunion of former POWs of Stalag Luft III, showing how during the war the company concealed maps between the front and back of playing cards for distribution by MIS-X.

Left: Display illustrating how a map concealed in playing cards like that shown above would have worked.

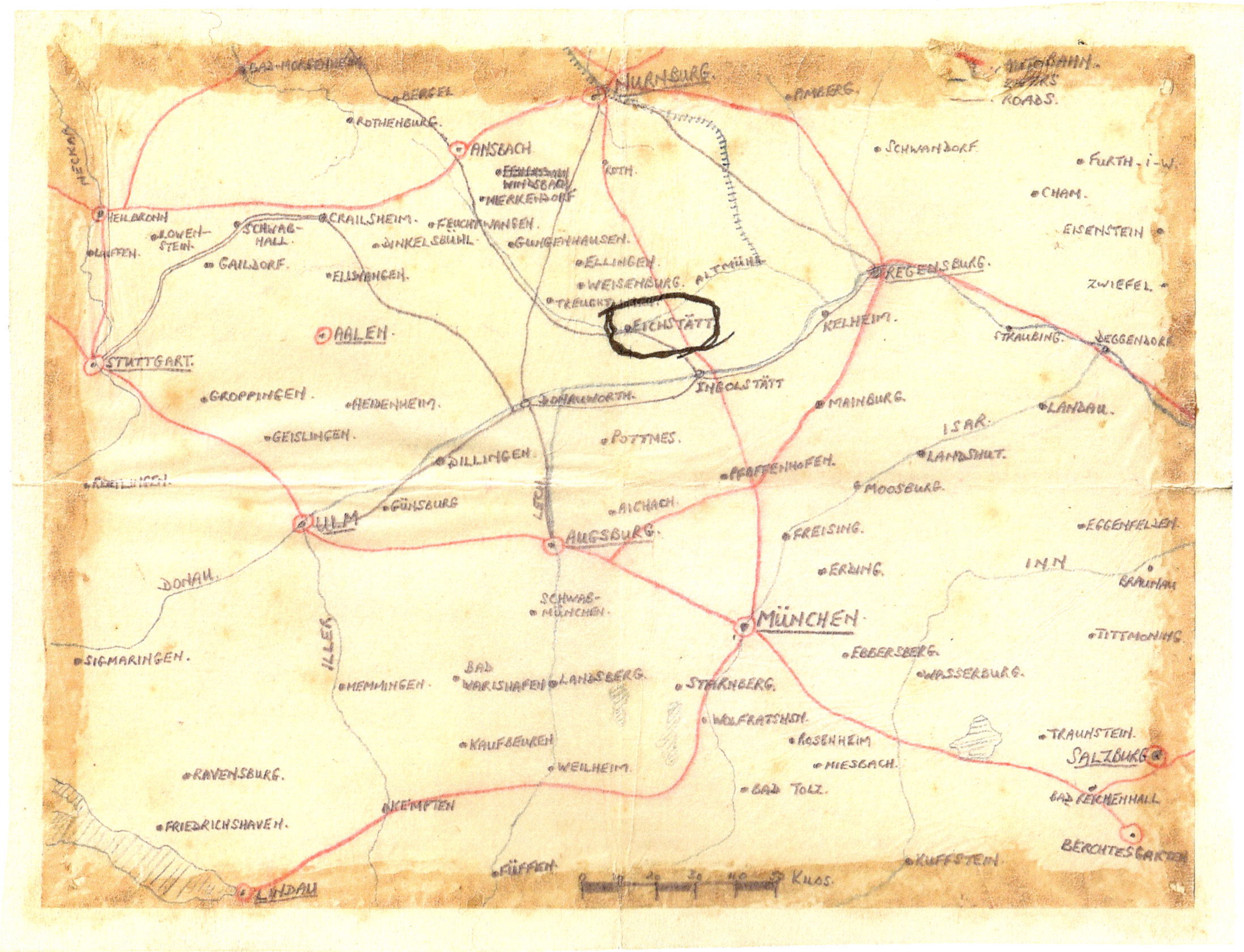

Official escape maps were not taken on escapes from camps lest they be discovered, so copies of maps were drawn by prisoners for use upon escape. This map of the vicinity around Oflag VIIB at Eichstatt was drawn (or traced) on tissue paper by John Symmons, RAF, who was interned at the prison. It was glued to another piece of paper after the war.

Above: Executives at R. J. Reynolds working after hours were able to secret escape aids in cigarette packs. This cut-away illustrates how easily tissue maps could be concealed.

Below: This display illustrates how compasses could easily be hidden inside cigarettes.

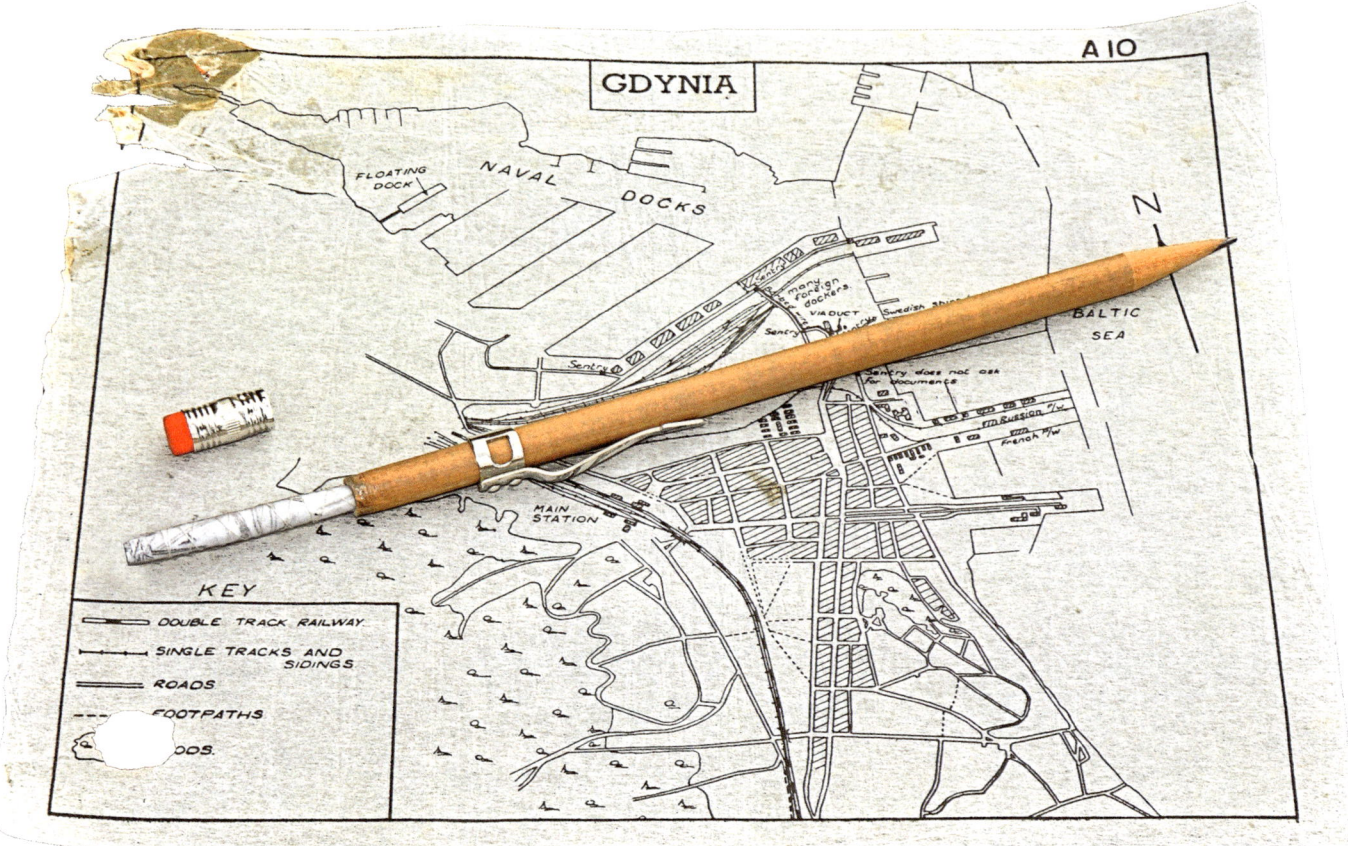

Authentic rice paper map sheet A10, of the harbor at Gdynia in Poland, with a display illustrating how it could be easily concealed in a pencil by rolling and wrapping it in thread. The magnetized pencil clip is an escape compass hiding in plain sight.

Above left: This box of German matches was acquired in 1969 from a Mr. Kalish, an AAF veteran who was interred in Stalag Luft III. He wrapped it with a letter and sealed it with red wax in camp to make it waterproof. The camp was liberated before this could be used upon escape.

Above Right: This shaving brush from RCAF veteran Howard Bond, has been loaded to illustrate how aids could be easily secreted by servicemen in such an item. The tissue map and compass in the cap easily fits into the handle containing German currency. An escape aid from MI9 would not open by simply unscrewing it.

Right: This British shaving kit illustrates how German currency could be concealed in the handle of a razor. The handle in a similar kit from MI9 would not be so easy to open.

RAF 1943 Pattern Escape Boots were designed so that the evader could cut off the uppers, allowing him to wear less conspicuous street shoes. A knife for this purpose was supplied in a special pocket inside the boot.

Detail showing end of folding knife sticking out of its special pocket inside the boot uppers.

The folding knife that was supplied with Escape Boots was as simple and functional as they come. It is shown along with worn black lace with corroded metal tips typical of the period illustrating how by war's end a medical bone saw, known as a Gigli Saw, was concealed inside escape boot laces.
Special thanks to Mick Prodger who provided the knife on loan for this exhibition.

To all Prisoners of War!

The escape from prison camps is no longer a sport!

Germany has always kept to the Hague Convention and only punished recaptured prisoners of war with minor disciplinary punishment.

Germany will still maintain these principles of international law.

But England has besides fighting at the front in an honest manner instituted an illegal warfare in non combat zones in the form of gangster commandos, terror bandits and sabotage troops even up to the frontiers of Germany.

They say in a captured secret and confidential English military pamphlet,

THE HANDBOOK OF MODERN IRREGULAR WARFARE:

". . . the days when we could practise the rules of sportsmanship are over. For the time being, every soldier must be a potential gangster and must be prepared to adopt their methods whenever necessary."

"The sphere of operations should always include the enemy's own country, any occupied territory, and in certain circumstances, such neutral countries as he is using as a source of supply."

England has with these instructions opened up a non military form of gangster war!

Germany is determined to safeguard her homeland, and especially her war industry and provisional centres for the fighting fronts. Therefore it has become necessary to create strictly forbidden zones, called death zones, in which all unauthorised trespassers will be immediately shot on sight.

Escaping prisoners of war, entering such death zones, will certainly lose their lives. They are therefore in constant danger of being mistaken for enemy agents or sabotage groups.

<u>Urgent warning is given against making future escapes!</u>

In plain English: Stay in the camp where you will be safe! Breaking out of it is now a damned dangerous act.

<u>The chances of preserving your life are almost nil!</u>

All police and military guards have been given the most strict orders to shoot on sight all suspected persons.

Escaping from prison camps has ceased to be a sport!

This large German poster appeared in POW camps in September 1944 to warn that escapers would be shot on sight. In fact, Germany had been pursuing this course for much of the year already. Of the 73 prisoners who were captured after the March 1944 "Great Escape" from Stalag Luft III, 50 were murdered. In mid 1944, 168 Allied evaders were captured in Paris, but instead of being sent to POW camps, the airmen were shipped to the notorious death camp at Buchenwald. In August 1944, the Allies acknowledged this troubling change in German behavior when they sent a coded message to all Stalags and Oflags that freed Allied officers from their obligation to escape.

The month that this German poster appeared in the camps, 47 Allied airmen were murdered within 48-hours of arriving at a POW camp in Mauthausen.

Epilogue

The number of escapers and evaders who returned to Allied control in all theatres of the Second World War is estimated at 35,847. Some 12,000 of these soldiers were American. The numbers are not exact, but they confirm the courage and fortitude of our service personnel. The numbers also emphasize the value of the E&E agencies that provided not only training and aids, but also a psychological edge to service personnel that came from knowing that there were people working secretly on their behalf.

Following VJ Day, all known records and artifacts of MIS-X were burned and the buildings that housed the agency were razed. Barely three years later, no useful information could be found when the USAF formed its Evasion and Escape Section. Britain kept files from MI9 secret for years following the war.

In the conflicts that followed World War II, evasion, and particularly escape once captured, became exponentially more dangerous. Airmen and special operations personnel continued to be trained, and they carried survival and E&E aids, but during the Korean War, the use of helicopters supported by aircraft became the primary means of rescuing people. It remains so today.

Today's survival, evasion, and escape aids, together with the modern Survival, Evasion, Resistance and Escape (SERE) training provided to today's armed services personnel, as well as their Search and Rescue (SAR) units, can trace their heritage directly to the noble and courageous people of the World War II evasion and escape agencies who unwaveringly served their men at arms behind enemy lines.

Guest Curator R. E. Baldwin is an independent scholar who has been researching and collecting evasion and escape material since 1985. His collection of language-related evasion and escape aids is considered definitive, and he is the acknowledged world authority on these aids. His collection of evasion and escape maps ranks among the world's most comprehensive among private collectors. He has penned dozens of periodical articles on evasion and escape aids, and is the lead author of *Last Hope: The Blood Chit Story* (Schiffer Publishing, 1997). He has given presentations to groups as diverse as aviation societies in the United States and small gatherings of artists in Japan. He curated the Fragile Hope exhibition of language aids and cloth maps shown for their design elements at the Design Museum of the University of California at Davis, California, in 2003. Mr. Baldwin is a civilian consultant to the National Museum of the United States Air Force.

www.ingramcontent.com/pod-product-compliance
Lightning Source LLC
Chambersburg PA
CBRC090903080526
44588CB00006B/79